THE JEWS IN ENGLAND

THE JEWS IN ENGLAND

A History for Young People

Beth-Zion Abrahams

VALLENTINE MITCHELL – LONDON

Grateful acknowledgement is made for the use of the following pictures :

The Petition of 1656 (facing p. 96) which is in the Public Record Office by kind permission of the Controller of H.M. Stationery Office.

The portrait of Sir David Salomons (facing p. 208) is reproduced from the David Salomons' House Catalogue of Mementoes.

The portrait of the Marquess of Reading by kind permission of the National Portrait Gallery, London.

"Baron de Rothschild admitted to the House of Commons" by H. Barraud (facing p. 209) by kind permission of N. M. Rothschild & Sons.

"Carrying the Law" by Sir William Rothenstein (facing p. 224) by kind permission of the Johannesburg Art Gallery.

First published by
Robert Anscombe & Co. Ltd., 1950

Second edition (revised) published 1969 by
Vallentine Mitchell & Co. Ltd.,
18 Cursitor Street, London E.C.4

© Beth-Zion Abrahams 1950, 1969

SBN 85303019 7

Set and printed in Great Britain by
Tonbridge Printers Ltd., Peach Hall Works,
Tonbridge, Kent

CONTENTS

Part II. THE MIDDLE PERIOD

Part III. THE MODERN PERIOD

LIST OF ILLUSTRATIONS

Part 1
THE EARLY PERIOD
From Roman Britain till 1290

IN ROMAN TIMES

Britain is now a civilized and highly developed country. It is hard to imagine that more than two thousand years ago this island was covered with dense forest and great stretches of marsh in which wild animals roamed.

Julius Caesar and other Romans who wrote of Ancient Britain describe the natives of these isles. They tell of their primitive way of living, how they dyed their skins with blue and green juices of plants to make them look fiercer in battle and so frighten their foes. We know from these Roman writers that the ancient Britons were just beginning to learn what was happening in the great world outside their island. Merchants came across the seas to trade their wares for tin which was a very precious metal and which was mined on the southern coast, in the part known today as Cornwall.

From distant lands came adventurous traders in their own ships. They were the Phoenicians who, long before that time had left their ancient home in Sidon and Tyre, on the coast of ancient Syria north of the Land of Israel, and settled in

Carthage which was in the region of North Africa now known as Tunisia.

These Phoenicians belonged to the same race as Hiram, king of Tyre, who helped king Solomon to build the first Temple in Jerusalem. They spoke a language very much like our own Hebrew tongue. We know that some of the Hebrew tribes who lived in the northern part of the Land of Israel close to the Phoenician border, the tribes of Dan and Zebulun, were seamen and traders also. So that it is possible that our ancestors were among the earliest traders to the far-off isles of Britain. They may have come here long before Julius Caesar set foot on the coast of Kent in the year 55 – before the common era. Jewish soldiers served in the Roman legions stationed in Britain, and were appointed officials during the 4th century.

In order to understand better how our fore-fathers came to seek homes in distant places be-yond the Land of Israel, we must go back long before the time when the very name of Britain appears in history.

More than twelve hundred years before Julius Caesar landed in Britain, our ancestors had already left Egypt and had wandered through the wilderness to the Promised Land. From that time until Britain appears in history, the Israelites had become a great nation: Moses had brought down

the Law from Mount Sinai, David had written
his psalms and our Hebrew prophets had brought
their message to the world.

But our nation, after prosperity, suffered two
great calamities.

The first calamity occurred about 500 years
before the Romans came to Britain, when the
Temple of Solomon was destroyed and a great
part of the Hebrew nation was taken into exile.
From that time onwards, Jews were to be found
in many lands and cities outside the Land of
Israel. They gradually spread throughout Asia,
North Africa and Southern Europe. But all this
time they looked towards Jerusalem as their
home. Those who were able to do so visited this
holy city at least once in their lifetime.

In the Land of Israel itself, the Jewish nation
meanwhile became strong again. About 300 years
after the first great calamity they were powerful
enough, under the great hero Judas Maccabeus,
to drive out the armies of Antiochus Epiphanes,
an event which we still celebrate every year
during the eight days of the Chanucah festival.

During this period the Roman empire was
growing fast. The Romans conquered country
after country, continuing their conquests until,
240 years after Judas Maccabeus, their armies
laid siege to Jerusalem, laid the second Temple
in ruins, and captured it after one of the bitterest

fights in history. This was the second calamity.

Once again great numbers of our ancestors were driven into exile. Many made their way to the lands and cities where their brethren already lived. Others were sold into slavery and taken to distant lands like Spain, Germany, Gaul and perhaps also Britain, which had in the meantime been conquered by the Romans.

In the city of Rome there stands to this day a monument known as the Arch of Titus. On this are shown the figures of the Jewish captives whom the Romans dragged in chains through the streets of Rome after the destruction of Jerusalem. It also shows the sacred vessels of the Temple which were taken as spoil by the Romans. To this very day, over 1800 years later, no patriotic Jew will pass under the Arch of Titus, but turns aside in grief and sorrow because of the ancient defeat which marked the beginning of the Diaspora – the Jewish exile.

It was about 120 years after the Romans first came to Britain that Jerusalem fell.

There was yet a third event that added to the great number of Jews who were by now scattered throughout the Roman dominions. It was the end of the great revolt under Bar Kochba when the Romans laid waste the Land of Israel and vast numbers of Jews were forced to seek refuge outside their homeland.

This last revolt was so fierce and desperate that the Romans were forced to bring to Judea – as they called the Land of Israel – their best general, Julius Severus, who was at that time governor of Britain. No doubt Julius Severus brought with him from Britain high officers, some of whom may even have been Britons, for we know that as time went on many Britons adopted the Roman customs and language and joined the Roman army. It may have been one of these who, having fought under Julius Severus in the war against Bar Kochba in Judea, returned home to Britain carrying with him jewels, money and other valuables which the victorious Roman soldiers were allowed to take with them. This may explain how one of the coins of the Jewish patriot Bar Kochba was found a few years ago by workmen digging on the site of the General Post Office in London; or how a coin struck in Gaza, in Judea, was found in Scotland.

We do not know this for certain; the Bar Kochba coin may have reached England by way of trade, through one of the Jewish traders, or Phoenician merchants, whom we have already mentioned.

The defeat of Bar Kochba marked the end of Jewish independence. The Temple, centre of Jewish worship, no longer existed and Jerusalem, the Holy City, was destroyed. The beautiful country of Israel had been laid in ruins by the Romans. From then onwards, Jews who had gone to foreign lands and lived in the Diaspora no longer expected to return to the land of Israel for many years to come. Wherever they lived in these lands, there they settled and made their homes. They dwelt side by side with the tribes who had by now passed out of savagery and became citizens of the Roman Empire.

THE LIGHT OF THE LAW

Though Jews had lost their country, they did not disappear among the nations with whom they dwelt for when they were exiled they carried with them the faith of their forefathers and the Holy Law, the Torah which was henceforth the guide of their life. We are told that when the Temple was destroyed, Vespasian, the commander of the Roman armies, allowed Rabbi Jochanan ben Zakkai to set up in Palestine a school for teaching the Torah and the Jewish traditions. Similar schools sprang up in most of the countries wherever Jews were scattered. The heads of these schools were learned men, renowned for their wisdom and their knowledge of the Torah.

Many of the lands of the exile were far from civilized. Some of them were very much like ancient Britain as described in the last chapter. Others were a little better; but only in Italy, Greece, and what is now known as the Middle East, was there any large number of people who could read and write or had any idea of the great world outside their own little cities and villages.

It was among these backward peoples that our

forefathers now made their homes. Of course, they were far above their neighbours in knowledge and education. Every Jewish boy and many of the Jewish girls could read and write. In countries where most people had never heard of a school for general education, Jews established their own schools. Children were brought up from early youth to understand the Jewish faith and to know the difference between their own way of life and that of their neighbours.

For the most part, the neighbours of our ancestors in countries like Ancient Britain, Gaul and Germany were pagans. They worshipped idols, or believed in gods of the woods and streams, of thunder and lightning. They had many such gods. To some of these gods they even sacrificed human beings. Indeed, the Druids who were the priests of pagan Britain and Gaul celebrated special festivals by burning alive numbers of human beings in great wicker cages.

Far different was the faith of our ancestors, the same faith that we follow today. The Jewish faith commands belief in the one God. Idols may not be worshipped. Not only has human sacrifice always been forbidden to us, but even the slightest cruelty to animal or human is prohibited.

About a hundred years after Britain was first invaded by the Roman army of Julius Caesar, a great change began to come over the pagan world. A new religion, Christianity, the founders of which were Jews born in the Land of Israel, began to spread. They believed that by allowing the pagans to keep some of their old beliefs and adding to these some of the higher teachings of the Jewish faith, they would gradually be able to bring the pagans to a higher state.

The new Christian religion was spread among the pagans by its early teachers or missionaries, most of whom were once Jews. But these missionaries did not all agree amongst themselves. Some wanted more of the Jewish teachings in their new faith, while others wanted more paganism. Some wanted to keep the seventh day as the Sabbath, according to the fourth Commandment; others wanted Sunday as the Sabbath, because Sunday was holy to the sun-god of the pagans. Some of these Jewish missionaries insisted on pagan converts to the Christian faith keeping all the Jewish laws, the Jewish festivals and the commandments concerning kosher food. Others were against this and allowed their converts to keep their old pagan festivals under new names, and eat all that their hearts desired.

For about 500 years this struggle between these two kinds of Christianity continued. But as time went on, the side which put fewer burdens on the pagans won. From then onward Christianity became so different and separate from the Jewish faith that Jews were even persecuted by the Christians who tried to prove that their religion was superior to the Jewish faith.

The ancient Britons had no system of writing such as we understand it today. They had a rude alphabet which only few could read or write. It was made up of notches cut into stone, or of twisted lines looking like twigs. It was the Romans who first brought to them a knowledge of the alphabet, in the same way as it was the ancient Hebrew alphabet that first led up to the Greek and later to the Roman or Latin alphabet.

But when the pagan Britons came to know the new religion, it became necessary for them to be able to read so that they might study and understand our Bible. The original language of the Bible, as you know, is Hebrew. In early times it was translated into the languages of different countries. The same happened in Britain, where after the Roman conquest British converts to Christianity studied Hebrew, Latin or Greek, in order to be able to read the Bible.

In the early monasteries of Britain, there were Bibles in Hebrew and other languages, but though the converts to Christianity owed a great part of their religion to the Hebrew Bible they did not always show gratitude for the fact that the founders of their religion were Jews.

You must remember all this and bear it in mind when you picture to yourself the Britain of that time when the pagan population was being gradually converted to Christianity.

You must also remember that the real cause of the triumph of Christianity over paganism was the Jewish teaching and the Bible, without which there could be no Christianity. It was the light of the Law and the teaching of the Prophets that drove the darkness out of pagan Britain as out of the other pagan countries in those days.

Remembering this, we may be justly proud that it was the teachings of our ancestors that first set the nations of those days moving along the path of civilization.

WILLIAM THE CONQUEROR 1066–1087

As we have seen, Jews must have been in Britain from very early times. Nevertheless, the first written records concerning Jews in this country begin only with the coming of William the Conqueror. This Norman king united all England under his strong rule. He came from France, part of ancient Gaul, where Jews had dwelt for many centuries. There they were merchants and traders, the link between the Western world and that world of the East whence came spices and silks. They had helped in making Gaul prosperous by their trading activities.

What wonder then that when William of Normandy defeated Harold at the Battle of Hastings and was crowned king of England, he invited Jews to come over and help in making the land prosperous? He divided the conquered land among his barons who had fought at his side and helped him to gain victory. The land was further divided among the lesser nobles who swore loyalty each to his own baron. They in turn owned smaller plots of land which were worked by Saxon thralls who were called serfs.

The towns were few in number and small in those days. Travel between the different towns and distant parts of the country was difficult, for roads were few and bad, and much of the land was covered by forests. There was very little trade. In fact there was scarcely any trade at all such as we have today. What trade there was often consisted of barter, that is, of exchange. For example, a man who had an article he did not need would exchange it for a pair of shoes or other article of which he was in need.

The greater part of the population were serfs who were compelled to live and work for the master under whom they were born. They received no wages in money, but the master had to provide them with dwelling, food and clothing. Money passed only between the lords of the manor and the townspeople, most of whom belonged to guilds which were the societies of tradesmen. Each trade or craft had its own guild. These tradesmen were paid in money. There was little export or import of goods.

William the Conqueror invited French Jews from Rouen to come to England for the purpose of trade. They came in fair numbers, bringing with them their own great experience in commerce.

Thus, the Jews made it possible for trade to progress. If a man wanted clothes he did not need to bring an animal, or a load of hay, or something else, to exchange or barter for clothes. He would bring money and pay in coin. It was better also for the king, for now his lords and barons paid their taxes in money. It was easier all round, and just as today banks are to be found wherever trade is done, so Jews were to be found in those times in all centres of trade. Indeed, they were the bankers of that age. Unlike the serfs, the thralls and the small farmers, they could travel freely about the country.

By their means the king found it easier to raise and collect the taxes of the country. Jews were placed under the king's special protection and thus they did not belong to this great lord, or to that great baron. While the serfs were each under their special lords of the manor, and the lords of the manor under the barons, the Jews were solely under the king and they were called his chattels.

There was no Bank of England in those days. Indeed, there were no banks at all such as we know them. Nowadays a bank has two duties: it looks after people's money safely, and it also lends money for business. In exchange for such loans, the banks charge what is known as interest, meaning that the person who borrows the money has to repay to the bank an agreed amount more for every pound that he has borrowed.

In William the Conqueror's time, it was thought wrong to take interest for money lent to anyone. This was so because the early Christians had accepted one of the commandments in our Hebrew Bible which forbade the taking of interest, or usury as it is called in the Bible. Our ancestors themselves had in the course of time made a difference between interest which was too high and interest which they thought reasonable. Experience had taught them that a reasonable interest was just and that without it most people would never lend any money. Trade dependent on profit, which is itself a kind of interest, would thus be impossible.

Now the English Christians, too, saw in the course of time that the commerce of the country could not progress unless loans were made possible and interest was allowed. Although there were Christians engaged in the giving of loans for trade, they preferred the Jews to do it. It was because of this that the Jews became the great bankers of that period. The lords of the manor would borrow money from the Jewish bankers in order to pay their taxes to the king or to buy certain luxuries which, coming from abroad, had to be paid for in coin accepted by foreign traders. The great monasteries would come to the Jewish bankers for money in order to build their fine abbeys and cathedrals. Indeed, records of those days prove that the building of some of the great cathedrals and castles of England was made possible by the Jewish bankers.

William the Conqueror reigned from 1066 to 1087. During these twenty-one years immense changes occurred in England. The country established a prosperous traffic with the rest of Europe. William was not only King of England, but also Duke of Normandy. The barons as well as the Jews who came over with him were men from the Continent of Europe. It was they who helped to change England from a remote island to a country in touch with the rest of the world.

The Jews who came with William the Conqueror rendered a number of special services which may be summed up in the following way:

They brought with them a knowledge of foreign languages, especially the knowledge of Hebrew of which even English bishops knew very little, although Christianity is largely based on the Hebrew Bible.

The Jews of Normandy were in touch with much of the then known world. Above all, the Hebrew language was in common use among themselves for commercial purposes, so that a Jew travelling in any part of the world could always make himself understood to another Jew by using the Holy tongue. It will be realised, therefore, how great was the service which the Jews who came to England with William the Conqueror rendered in building up the foreign trade as well as the industry of the country.

The great doctors and scientists of those days were mainly Jews and Arabs. The Jews who came to England brought with them the knowledge of medicine. Many of them settled in Oxford, which very soon after the Conquest, became an important seat of learning, and there established a medical school.

Three places are known to have served in Oxford as places of learning owned by Jews in 1073. They were the Moyses Hall, Lombard's Hall, and Jacob's Hall.

Everyone knows that William after he conquered England, ordered the making of the Domesday Book, a complete record of all the land property of the country, and the names of the owners of those estates. Many years passed before the Book was completed, and by that time Jews were settled in many parts of England. However, the Domesday Book itself does not mention Jews by name, nor does it mention any other people by their nationality or religion.

WILLIAM RUFUS 1087–1100

William Rufus ascended the throne of England in 1087. His father William the Conqueror had been Duke of Normandy as well as King of England, but he had left Normandy to the elder brother of Rufus. As we have seen in the last chapter, the first Jews of England came over from Normandy. They afterwards used to travel backwards and forwards between the two countries treating them almost as one. But as William Rufus was no longer the ruler of Normandy we may suppose that Jews were no longer as free to travel back and forth as formerly. Moreover Rufus from the very beginning of his reign waged many wars. He fought against the Welsh and the Scots, as well as against his elder brother Robert, the Duke of Normandy.

Rufus also kept a very costly court and spent a great deal of wealth on the men and women who made up his retinue.

In order to pay for the cost of his wars and his expensive court, Rufus made use of his Jewish bankers. But unlike some of the later kings who ill-treated the Jews while using their money,

Rufus was friendly to them. This may have been because he did not wish to risk the Jews escaping out of England to Normandy and thus enriching his brother.

Rufus was also throughout his reign in dispute with the French. The Pope tried to take away from him the power of choosing the heads of the Church in England. This resulted in a feud between the Church and Rufus. The outcome was that the monks who wrote the history of that time disliked him and described him as a bad king who frittered away his time in hunting and other pastimes.

We must remember that it required a great deal of courage even for a king to stand up against the Church in those days. Rufus well knew how powerful the Church was, and that in some countries it was actually strong enough to depose kings and emperors.

One example of the stories that the monks told against Rufus is the following tale. They relate that many Jews in Rouen, a part of Normandy which Rufus had meantime regained from his brother, had gone over to the Christian religion. The monks, in order to blacken Rufus in the eyes of Christians and future generations, then go on to tell us that Rufus was bribed by other Jews to force them back to the Jewish faith. The actual truth is that the first Crusade was then in progress. Many Jews were slain by the Crusaders on their way to the Holy Land. In Rouen Jews were driven into a church by the Crusaders and baptized at the point of the sword. Later, Rufus allowed them to return to the faith of their fathers. But monkish writers invented their own story which contained two falsehoods: first, that the Jews had been baptized of their own free will; second, that Rufus, after being bribed, forced them back to the Jewish faith against their will.

In those days the Church was anxious to convert Jews to Christianity; in most cases using force to do so.

But not all the churchmen were so cruel. Others tried to persuade Jews by discussion or by attempting to prove the truth of the Christian faith from Jewish writings. One such discussion took place in London. The only accounts of the time come from Christian writers who tell us that Rufus brought together Jews and Christians in a public debate. They relate that king Rufus declared in jest 'By the face of Luke', that he himself would become a Jew if the Jews overcame the Christians in a discussion. The discussion is claimed by the Christian writers as ending in a victory for the Christians. But indeed, they confess that the Jews themselves complained that they were beaten by force and not by argument.

13th century House in Lincoln traditionally known as Aaron the Jew's House

Group of Jews (right) and Christians. Note the characteristic
Jewish hat worn by Jews during the Middle Ages

These public disputes took their rise with the Crusades. The Crusades were holy wars proclaimed by the Church against the Saracens who held Jerusalem and the Holy Land. The Christians were grieved that the Holy Land, where the founder of their faith was buried, should be in the hands of the Saracens (the name the medieval Christians gave to the Moslems), whom they called infidels or unbelievers. They therefore called upon barons, knights and others to forsake their homes and form armies for conquering the Holy Land. In order to persuade as many as possible to join, the Pope proclaimed that all who joined in the Crusade would have their sins forgiven. Some of those who went on the Crusades were pious and holy men who were really distressed because their holy places were in the hands of the Saracens: others were cruel and bloodthirsty, seeking only adventure and loot.

Among the great lords who went on the Crusades was Duke Robert of Normandy, brother of William Rufus. But before he departed he sold the dukedom to his brother, and so Normandy once again became the possession of the king of England. Once more the Jews of England and Normandy were under the same ruler.

HENRY I 1100–1135

Rufus lost his life whilst hunting in the New Forest on the 2nd August, 1100, and was succeeded by his brother King Henry I.

When Henry I came to the throne, Jews in many countries outside England had suffered indescribable disaster. The first Crusade which started in 1096, five years before the death of Rufus, had run its course, and ended with the capture of the Holy Land. All the Jews who were found in Jerusalem at the time of its capture by the Crusaders were driven into the synagogues and burnt alive. The Crusaders who had started with the murder and pillage of many Jewish communities in Europe ended their crusade in this savage manner in Jerusalem. Fortunately, at the time, Rufus was king of England and he ruled firmly and wisely; the Jews were permitted to live and work peacefully. Indeed, the number of Jews in England increased and we may suppose that some of the newcomers were refugees from the massacres in Europe.

Nevertheless, even in Europe not all was suffering and pain. In the midst of sorrows, the

Jews of France, Germany, Italy and Spain pursued their learning and studies. In France, there lived the celebrated scholar known as Rashi, a name formed out of the Hebrew initials of his full title which was Rabbenu Shlomo ben Yitzchak, that is: Our Master, Solomon son of Isaac. He is remembered as the man who explained the Bible and the writings of the Rabbis so clearly that even today no learned Jew would think of studying these Hebrew works without the help of Rashi's commentary.

To the Jews of England all these countries were hardly foreign lands. They sent their sons abroad to study under the great Rabbis, and letters passed frequently between them. We know that English Jews often sent to the great Rabbis on the Continent letters asking advice on matters connected with Jewish Law, and the replies that came back were obeyed with greater zeal than if they had come from an emperor.

But the Jews of England did not need to draw all their learning from abroad. In England, too, there were great Jewish schools and colleges to which Jewish boys were sent. In order that there should be sufficient teachers and rabbis for the congregations, every Jewish family gave one of its sons fully to the study of the Torah. In this the Jews of England followed the model of Jews in other countries.

Jewish learning was feared by the Church. Especially so, as Jews were so well versed in the original scriptures and their training in the great Hebrew schools gave them every advantage over their non-Jewish neighbours when discussing the Bible and religion.

By the year 1109, the Jews in different parts of England are said to have taught the Jewish faith and preached it to their Christian neighbours. The abbot Joffred of Croyland sent monks to London, Bristol, Norwich, York, Oxford, Cambridge and Stamford, the chief towns where Jews lived, on missions to strengthen Christians in their faith.

It was in this reign that there was issued what is known as the Jewish Charter. This made clear to the Jews and their neighbours the rights of the Jews. These rights had grown up gradually, and Henry I, called the 'Lion of Justice', collected all these into a special charter so that there could not be any doubts about them. The charter confirmed the right of Jews to move freely about the country. It allowed them to hold the land of people owing them money until the debt was repaid; it freed them from ordinary taxes, which meant that they could be taxed only by the king, and that such taxation went straight into the king's treasury. The Charter forbade the barons to ill-treat the Jews. It also gave to Jews the right of trial by a jury composed half of Jews and half of Christians. As the original charter has been lost, we do not know what else it contained. We only know that it served as a model for the charters that came later.

THE PIPE ROLLS

Although the Charter of Henry I confirmed the right of the Jews, it does not give us a complete picture of the Jewish position. In order to obtain this we must study the laws passed concerning the Jews under the different kings. Fortunately, in England, there were, from William the Conqueror's time onward, strong kings who did not allow the barons too much power. It was quite different in other countries, such as France and Germany, where the kings were weak and the barons and the town councils sometimes acted like independent sovereigns. In these countries, the Jews were often at the mercy of the barons and the rulers of the cities who did what they liked, taxing, ill-treating or expelling the Jews at will.

Henry's charter was given, not because the king had any special liking for the Jews, but because he wished to use the Jews for raising money for the country. His charter protected them against the barons, because he wished to make sure that none of the wealth of the Jews passed into their hands instead of his own. He allowed Jews to live freely in different parts of the country, not because he wished to give them freedom, which was not enjoyed by other Englishmen, but because he desired them to be spread about the country so that they could continue their business activities and thus make the profits from which the king himself took the greatest share. And when he allowed them to own lands, it was not because he wished to put them on the same level as the lords of the manors, but in this way he enabled them to take the lands of different people in pledge for money lent to them. Thus, they could carry on business with greater success for the king's profit.

All this is known to us through a wonderful collection of ancient records known as the Pipe Rolls. No one is sure why this name was given to these records, though some say it is because the parchments on which the records are written, when rolled up and placed on their shelves, look like stacked pipes. Parchment, as you know, is really the skin of animals, scraped and softened until it looks like very strong paper. It was used by the scribes of those days for writing on, as we use paper today.

There are still in existence very many such rolls. The oldest dates from the year 1130. The parchment skins on which they are written are usually about a yard long and fourteen inches in width. It so happens that the very oldest of the Pipe Rolls makes mention of our Jewish ancestors in England.

The Pipe Rolls are also sometimes called the Great Rolls of the Exchequer. This name really explains to us the true meaning of these records, and why these parchments were so guarded. The word 'Exchequer' means treasury. In actual fact the title 'Great Rolls of the Exchequer' signifies that all these parchments are nothing more nor less than the accounts of the taxation which the kings levied on the country. Thus, as the Jews were permitted to stay in England only because they were of use to the king for raising taxes for his exchequer, it is natural that the great Rolls of the Royal Exchequer should mention a great deal about the business affairs of the Jews.

And, indeed, it is so; for without these Pipe Rolls, or Great Rolls of the Exchequer as some call them, we would now know very little of the history of the Jews in England of these early days. They form a historic record of the period and are today part of Britain's national treasure.

From the Pipe Rolls we learn a number of very interesting things. The main facts they teach are:

1. The true position of the Jews and how they were treated.

2. The names of the most celebrated and important Jews who lived in England in those days, the towns and even the streets and houses in which some of them resided, the manner in

which the different kings treated their Jews, despite the Charter of Rights of Henry I, and the vast sums of money which Jews paid into the Royal treasury.

Some of these facts are of great interest and we shall therefore deal with them in separate chapters.

STEPHEN AND A LYING CHARGE
1135–1154

After the death of Henry I, his nephew Stephen was crowned king and civil war divided the land, for Henry's daughter Matilda claimed the throne. The barons fought some on one side and some on the other. It was a time of turmoil and unrest for the country. Jews, though they were not permitted to bear arms, did not escape the turmoil. When the barons, in 1136, set fire to London, the quarter where Jews lived suffered greatly, for in those days houses were built of wood and fires spread rapidly from house to house.

In the continuous fighting throughout the country, Stephen, harassed for ready cash, raised money from the Jews. When a certain Jew, Isaac of Oxford, refused to pay the sum demanded of him, the thatched roof of his house was set alight and he perished in the flames. In the same year, the town of Oxford changed hands twice. When Matilda's army was in control they extorted money from the Jews of that city. When Stephen recaptured the town, he demanded from the Jews three-and-a-half times as much as they had given Matilda. With the terrible example of Isaac before them, the Oxford Jews, to save themselves, were forced to submit to these heavy demands.

The country was in a lawless state. The barons, fearful for their own safety, built castles on their lands, stone forts against assault. In order to be able to do this, they raised money from the Jews. In fact many of the stately castles of England were built with Jewish money, as were also some of the great cathedrals and monasteries which stand to this very day, beautiful, lasting monuments of the times.

But for us Jews, the most outstanding event of Stephen's reign was the terrible charge known as Ritual Murder which was brought against the Jews of Norwich in the year 1144. It was an accusation which was the first of its kind, though, alas, not the last; for the lying charge of Ritual Murder has been brought forward time and time again in our history and has been the direct cause of the death of thousands of innocent people. It is sad indeed, that the shameful charge of Ritual Murder against Jews was first uttered in England.

'Ritual Murder' means murder for religious purposes. Enemies of Jews had invented the lie that Jews use Christian blood for celebrating Passover. In actual fact this charge was first invented and used against the early Christians at a time when the pagans were supreme.

In March, 1144, a little boy, William by name,

who lived in Norwich, was missed from his home and a hue and cry was raised. Search was made for him and his dead body was found in a nearby wood.

As was natural, there was much talk. One person had seen the boy in one place, another had seen him somewhere else. Someone said he had seen him entering the house of Eleazer the Jew, whereupon William's uncle accused the Jews of murdering William.

Then came the accusation by a certain Theobald of Cambridge who, it is sad indeed to relate, was a Jew by birth. This Theobald had changed his religion and become a monk. He was regarded by all Jews as a renegade or traitor. In order to revenge himself on his former brethren, Theobald declared that it was the custom of Jews to sacrifice a gentile child every Passover. He went on to say that a meeting was held every year when lots were cast to decide which town was to be chosen as the place for the murder, and at the meeting held that year in Narbonne, in France, the choice had fallen on Norwich.

A clamour arose for the arrest of the Jews of Norwich. One church claimed the boy as a martyr, calling him St William of Norwich. Pilgrimages began to be made to his tomb and riches poured into the cathedral where his body lay.

The Royal Sheriff was informed of what had happened. But this just man refused to arrest the Norwich Jews.

No Jew was arrested. No Jew was tried or convicted for this supposed murder, for there was no evidence that any Jew of Norwich or any other place had committed such a foul deed. In fact, an ancient chronicle relates that the boy had died of a fit and had not been murdered at all.

But the mischief had been done, a mischief which has, alas, caused terrible suffering for Jews throughout the centuries, down to modern times.

Without a single exception all accusations against Jews of ritual murder are false; and the charge that Jews use Christian blood for celebrating the Passover or any other festival is a lie and slander spread by our enemies.

Although Stephen is called a weak king, he now bestirred himself to protect the Jews. A Hebrew chronicle of that period gratefully records this fact, declaring that he would not allow them to be molested in person, or property, thus making possible the prosperity they were to enjoy in the next reign.

HENRY II 1154–1189

The reign of Henry II marked the most prosperous period for the English Jews of that age. Under the strong rule of this king, the land enjoyed peace. The civil war which had marred Stephen's reign was now at an end, and the whole country was united under Henry. London in those days, it was said, was the most French town in Europe. Besides being king of England and Duke of Normandy, Henry was lord of Anjou, of Poitou, Brittany and Gascony. The king of France in those days was king of but a small portion of that land.

Henry was the first of the line known as Angevin, so called from the district of Anjou and Jews of this period are referred to as Jews of Angevin England.

In Henry's French domains there were large settlements of Jews. These were in constant touch with their brethren across the English Channel. This was an easy matter for them for, apart from the Hebrew tongue which they used in their religious and business letters, they spoke French among themselves. This was the language

46

of the Court, the knights, the barons and the ruling classes, while the serfs and ordinary citizens spoke the Saxon tongue.

The common use of French by the Jews of Angevin England is illustrated by a story told by the monkish historian Giraldus Cambrencis. It also shows the friendly relations existing between Jews and their neighbours. About the year 1155 a certain Jew journeyed to Shrewsbury in company with the Archdeacon of Malpas whose name was Peché, the French word meaning sin, and a deacon whose name was Deville. On reaching a steep narrow part, called Bad Place, the Archdeacon remarked that his deanery started here at Bad Place and extended to Malpas, which means Bad Pass, near Chester. Glancing at his two companions the Jew reflected and then made the following witty remark: 'Is it so? God grant me a safe journey in this part, whose Archdeacon is Sin (Peché), whose dean is the Devil, which you enter through a Bad Place and go out in a Bad Pass.'

Henry's ascent to the throne marked the full restoration of order in the country. The ancient chronicles tell us that merchants once more came out from behind the safety of the city walls and great stone castles in quest of commerce.

The Pipe Rolls of these early years show that Jews were already spread throughout the country.

There was no town of importance where they were not to be found, each community having its own synagogue and school.

The most marked event during the early years of Henry's reign was the visit to England of Abraham ibn Ezra, the great Hebrew scholar and writer. He was born in Spain in 1092. In those days Spain was the great centre of Jewish learning. From it came scholars, poets and men of science who spread learning throughout Europe. Despite the dangers of travel, they journeyed far afield to become acquainted with distant lands and exhanged knowledge with the Jewish scholars in remote cities. It was on one of these journeys that Abraham ibn Ezra made his famous visit to London. The visit is known to us because he mentions it in a book which he wrote during his stay in London in May, 1158. His work gives us interesting information of the learning of the English Jews of those days.

It was about the year 1166 that Jews began to be employed by the king as Fern-gatherers, that is, collectors of taxes. Henry having borrowed much money from the Jewish bankers, instead of paying them back directly permitted them to collect the debts he owed them from the taxes due to him. This was afterwards one of the reasons for the great unpopularity of the Jews for tax-gatherers are never popular.

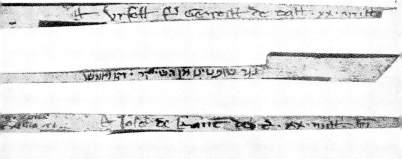

Shetaroth, or starrs written in Hebrew dated 1253. see pp. 54 and 69

Hebrew tallies of the thirteenth century. see p. 71

Menasseh ben Israel. Etching by Rembrandt

Between them and the Church at this time good relationship existed, as is shown by the following incident told by the historians.

On one occasion, there were gathered in St Paul's Church, London, many bishops and abbots to discuss certain letters sent by the Pope. Now, in those days, the land surrounding St Paul's, as well as part of the ground of the church itself, including the courtyard, served as a market. Stalls and booths were erected and there was always a throng of people present, some for business, others to meet their friends, and some out of idle curiosity.

At this particular meeting of the bishops and abbots, it chanced that some London Jews entered the courtyard to see whether they could meet certain people. Among them was Deodatus, the then Chief Rabbi of the Jews of London, who was popularly called the Bishop of the Jews.

On seeing Deodatus, someone in the crowd called out in a hearty voice, 'Welcome, Bishop of the Jews!' and turning to the priests about him, said 'Welcome and receive him among you, for there is hardly one among all you present who has not betrayed, at some time or another, your head, the Archbishop of Canterbury. But never this Bishop. In this Jewish Bishop there is, indeed, no disobedience!'

Apart from providing loans for the building

D

of fine monasteries and castles, Jews were the first to build stone houses. Up to this time houses had been built of wood, the roofs of which were thatched and so caught fire easily. The oldest stone house in England, still existing, is that known to this very day as the Jew's House, in Lincoln. It is also called Aaron of Lincoln's House, after its first owner about whom you will soon read.

In the year 1168 the second charge of Ritual Murder was brought against English Jews. At the Passover time of that year, several Jews had met in Gloucester in celebration of the circumcision of the son of a leading member of the community in that city. Again there was the terrible charge, the false accusation that they had met for the purpose of torturing a Christian child in order to obtain his blood for religious purposes. They were accused of having done to death a child named Harold and thrown his body into the river. This was not, unfortunately, the last of these false charges. In fact, in the reign of Henry, at the time when Jews were enjoying their greatest prosperity, there were several such false accusations of which, however, no Jew was proved guilty. Nor could be, for ritual murder is not and has never been a part of our religion.

Nowadays, looking back on what happened after these false accusations, we can understand what brought them about. The church or cathedral where the body of the supposed victim was buried, was visited as a place of pilgrimage. The worshippers brought rich gifts which they left for the monks and the priests. This led wicked men to encourage these shameful charges against the Jews: for the churches without such pilgrimages coveted the wealth which had come to other churches.

But being under the king's protection the Jews of that period did not suffer then so greatly from these false accusations as they might otherwise have done, or indeed, as they afterwards did suffer.

Mention has already been made, of the house of Aaron of Lincoln, the oldest stone house still inhabited in England. This Aaron of Lincoln, who was born about 1125, was the leading banker of his day. Among the abbeys and cathedrals built by means of the money he lent, and standing today, marvels of architecture, are the Abbey of St Albans and the Cathedrals of Peterborough and Lincoln. Aaron had business dealings not only with the heads of the Church, but with the king of Scotland, apart from the great English nobles. The growing towns of Southampton and Winchester borrowed money from him; and so extensive was his business that he had his agents – fellow Jews – in every part of the country, just as big modern banks have their branches all over the land.

When Aaron died in 1186, he was the wealthiest person in the country. This was too good an opportunity for the king to miss, and he took possession of all that Aaron had left, declaring his rights to this on the ground that the goods of a chattel belonged to his master. All the gold and jewels Henry sent to France to subsidise the war he was then waging – but the whole of this treasure was lost at sea. The remainder of Aaron's fortune was so great that a special branch of the Exchequer was set up to deal with it. Two treasurers and two clerks were appointed to keep the accounts of the debts owing to Aaron of Lincoln which were now collected for the king.

Under Henry II, English Jews enjoyed a period of quiet activity. They lived for the most part on friendly terms with their gentile neighbours. It was to this period that the first Shetar, that of Aaron of Lincoln, belongs: that is, a document in Hebrew, showing that money owing has been repaid. These Shetaroth, called Starrs in English, were afterwards so numerous that they were kept in a special chamber of the Exchequer. This room was later called the Star Chamber and is well known in English history for the great decisions that were taken there. The name comes from the Hebrew word Shetar.

The London Jews of those days, came not only from France, but from places as far away as Morocco, Spain and even Kiev in Russia.

When in 1188 the Jews were taxed £60,000, about a quarter of their wealth, by Henry II, the rest of the population gave only a tenth part of theirs, that is £70,000. Though the Jews were a minute fraction of the population, a twelfth part of the whole yearly income of the state came from Jewish sources. It was because of the wealth brought to his Exchequer through the Jews that the king quarrelled with the clergy who strove for Jewish conversion. Henry knew that if a Jew became a Christian he, the king, would be the loser, as Christians were not supposed to engage in lending money at interest.

CORONATION DAY OF RICHARD I

With the death of Henry II, the period of freedom and prosperity ended for the Jews of England. From now on they became in very truth the king's chattels, a sponge to suck up money and be squeezed dry again by the reigning monarchs.

Richard I, sometimes called the Lion-hearted, came to the throne in 1189. He was a stern man and before he became king had taken the pledge to go on a Crusade. When a prince he had fought against his own father.

The very beginning of his reign was marked by a terrible massacre, when the blood of innocent Jews flowed as a result of prejudice and hatred. The occasion was the coronation of Richard, while he was being crowned at Westminster Abbey. Richard who was superstitious and had taken oath to go on the Crusades, ordered that no women or Jews should be present at his coronation. Now, it is usual, whenever a new king is crowned, for representatives of the different communities in a country to be present, to offer their congratulations and greetings, bringing with them gifts to present to the new monarch.

More than any other people, the Jews wished to bring greetings and expressions of loyalty to the new king, knowing full well that if they did not present themselves they – and indeed all Jews – would be suspected of disloyalty. So the leading Jews of England assembled, choosing from among them those who were to bear their loyal greetings to Richard and to offer him costly gifts.

They arrived at Westminster Abbey only to find they were not allowed to enter the court-yard and thus were forced to mingle with the crowds of sightseers standing about the gates. There was some pushing in the crowd and two of the Jews were pushed through the gates. The men on duty, squires of the knights who were within the Abbey forecourt attending at the coronation ceremony, seeing the Jewish leaders within the gates, began to beat them and thrust them out. The crowd wanted little excuse to follow this treatment. They too, attacked the Jewish leaders with staves and stones. The crowd, come to witness a crowning, stayed to enjoy a riot against innocent men. They struck at them, they beat them with cudgels and pursued those that fled, following them to their houses and plundering whatever they could.

Some of the strong stone Jewish houses with-stood the attacks, but the less fortunate Jews who lived in wooden houses had their thatched roofs set alight and were burnt to death within. Any Jew trying to escape was killed. Jewish blood flowed while Jewish cries filled the air. Some kindly Christian neighbours gave protection to Jews – but these were few. One or two Jews, among them the well-known Benedict of York, was forced at the sword's point to be baptized; others refused and were killed on the spot. Sad and bitter, indeed, for the Jews of England was the coronation day of Richard.

The king heard the tumult while he was banqueting. Learning the cause and remembering that Jews were his chattels and necessary for the money they brought into the Exchequer, he sent out knights to quell the disturbance. But the mob was too inflamed to stop. They rioted, murdered and plundered for twenty-six hours. When night came the flames from the burning Jewish houses served them with light for their devilish work.

The following day Benedict, who when baptized had been given the name of William, was brought before the king. 'Who art thou?' the king enquired of him. 'I am Benedict the Jew, from York,' he answered. Surprised at this answer from the newly-baptized Christian, Richard turned to the Archbishop of Canterbury who had brought him the tidings of the conversion of this wealthy leader of the York Jewish community. 'Did you not tell me that he had become a Christian?' he asked. The Archbishop answered 'Yes, sire.' Whereat Richard asked, 'What shall we do with him?' And the Archbishop, in a passion, cried, 'Since he does not wish to be a Christian let him go to the devil'. Thus the miserable Benedict was released. He died shortly afterwards at Northampton, on his way back to York, despised by his Jewish brethren for having denied the faith of Israel.

The king, angry at the rioting at his coronation, and the loss his Exchequer had suffered, ordered an inquiry. But the mob had dispersed and it was not possible to trace the leaders of the riot. Several persons were arrested. Three were hanged, though not because they had murdered Jews and pillaged Jewish property. One was hanged because he had, in the excitement, stolen the goods of a fellow Christian; and the other two because the fire they had applied to a Jewish home had spread and destroyed the house of a Christian neighbour.

Orders for the protection of his Jewish chattels, were sent by Richard to the sheriffs of the different counties. But this was of little avail. The crusading fever swept the country, affecting alike baron and knight, townsman and peasant. Rumours of Jewish wealth and the treasures that had been looted by the rioters spread. Others were eager to share the plunder, while the nobles, many of whom owed much money to the Jewish bankers, were equally keen to be rid of their debts.

Anti-Jewish outbreaks spread; houses were pillaged and burnt; Jews were murdered. In some cases Crusaders took part in these riots; in others barons led the mob. Norwich Jews fled for protection to the royal castle and found safety within its walls. Those who failed to reach the castle in time were brutally slaughtered. At Stamford, too, Jews sought and found safety in the castle.

It was a time of terror for English Jews. Alone among the leading cities, according to the chronicle of the time, Winchester spared her Jews. And though this happened many centuries ago, we must remember this with gratitude – and also those few good citizens who saved the lives of their Jewish neighbours by giving them shelter in time of trouble.

THE MARTYRS OF YORK

All the outbreaks and riots against Jews in the first months of Richard's reign were small events compared with the terrible massacre at York in March, 1190. The Jewish community in York was old and prosperous, and had sent two men to represent them at the king's coronation. One of them was Benedict of whom you have just read, the other was named Josce.

When Richard left for the Crusades, all the evil passions against Jews were loosed, and at York so fierce was the onslaught that scarcely one member of the community remained alive. The signal for the outbreak was an attack on the house of Benedict who had died at Northampton. His house was plundered and set on fire, and his wife and children perished in the flames. The Jews of York fled to the castle for safety, taking with them whatever possessions they could carry.

Men, women, old people, children and babes in arms, the whole Jewish community sheltered in the castle while their homes were destroyed and their goods pillaged. The news of the onslaught on the Jews in other cities had reached them.

They felt that only in the castle would they find safety. One day the governor of the castle was refused admittance. It is not known for certain what led the Jews to lock the castle gate against the governor. But it is thought they suspected that he was in league with the rioters and planned to drive them forth.

Be it as it may, the governor appealed to the sheriff who happened by chance to be in the city. The sheriff, supported by the leaders of the rioters in the town, agreed to use his soldiers against the poor, defenceless Jews who had fled to York castle. His forces were strengthened by the rabble who lusted for blood. A mighty number stormed the castle. As though they were arrayed against an army they brought up battering-rams to make a breach in the strong castle walls. Only the most respectable citizens held aloof and refused to take part.

The clergy joined the mob, encouraging them to action. One hermit, clothed in his white robes, was in the very front and urged the men in a loud voice, crying, 'Crush the enemies of Christ! Crush the enemies of Christ!' He approached closer to the wall, exhorting the mob to greater effort. A huge piece of rock pushed over the ramparts, struck him. He fell, crushed to death, the only one of the assailants to be killed.

Within the castle walls, without arms and without food, the Jews were in a hopeless plight. They were at the mercy of a pitiless mob. Well they knew that whatever they did, their fate would be a bitter one. Now, alas, at this sad time, they realized more than ever, that they were strangers in a strange land. In exile, indeed, without protection of a country of their own, and with no defence.

It was on a Friday evening, 16th March, 1190 the eve of the Great Sabbath, the name given to the Sabbath day before Passover – that the Jews of York suffered martyrdom. The leader of the community Rabbi Yomtov, a great scholar who had come from France to be rabbi of the York Jews, stood up. 'Men of Israel,' he exclaimed in a firm voice, 'the God of our fathers ... commands us at this time to die for His Law. Behold, death is before us, and it is only left to us to consider how to undergo it in the most honourable and easy way. If we fall into the hands of our enemies, which we cannot possibly escape, our deaths will be not only cruel, but dishonourable. They will torture us and slake their revenge with our blood. Therefore, let us surrender our lives, to our Creator ... be our own executioners. We do not need examples from our history, alas, to prove that it is lawful for us to do so. Our illustrious ancestors acted in this way on like occasions.'

The aged Rabbi spake thus bravely, and when he finished sat down and wept.

Some approved of what Rabbi Yomtov had said, whilst others disagreed. Whereat rising again, Rabbi Yomtov said, 'Brethren, seeing we are not all agreed, let those who do not agree depart from this assembly.' Some few went, but the vast majority remained with their leader.

They first set fire to their valuables, their costly garments, and utterly destroyed them so that nothing of value should fall into the hands of their enemies. Then took place the saddest and most terrible scene of all: Each Jew, taking a sharp knife in his hand, slew his own wife and then his children. Josce set the first example with his wife Anna, then took his own life. The dread scene continued till Rabbi Yomtov remained alone. Then with a loud voice, reciting the Jewish declaration of faith, the Shema: 'Hear, O Israel, the Lord our God is one God,' he took his own life.

Moved by the solemnity of the scene and heroism of the martyrs, those who had at first faltered were now strengthened. They too burnt their valuables and costly garments; they threw what the fire could not consume down the sinks and drains of the castle. Lacking the hardihood to follow the example of their brethren they set

JEWISH

Israel's j

THE UNITED NATIONS' conder

Rare double

The coincidence of Purim and February 29 falling on the same day (Tuesday) was an extremely rare occurrence. **Dr Bernard Homa**, one of whose hobbies is the study of the calendar (as of so many other things), tells me that it last happened 144 years ago (in 1828). It will not occur again for another 152 years (until 2124) provided, of course, that the civil calendar is not reformed in the meantime.

fire to the castle building in which they were, and perished in the flames.

A mere handful remained. After the slaughter and the fire, these terror-stricken people called from the ramparts. They told the assailants of what had happened, throwing the dead bodies of the martyrs over the walls to prove the truth of what they said. They offered to accept baptism if their lives were spared. Their lives were promised them on that condition. But they had no sooner lowered the drawbridge and opened the gates, than the rabble fell on them, and killed them. Not one remained alive, thus, indeed, proving the truth of Rabbi Yomtov's words.

From the castle, the mob made its way to the cathedral. Here for protection were kept the records of debts due to the Jews. They forced the keepers to deliver these to them. Piling up the records in a heap they set them alight, making a huge bonfire in the very cathedral itself. Then the mob dispersed and York returned to its normal existence.

But the Jewish community of York was no longer in being; all had been slain in sanctification of God's Holy Name.

The destruction of the records of the debts due roused Richard to great wrath on his return, for it meant that he was the loser. He ordered an inquiry and from the records of this which still exist, we have the names of many of those who took part in the York massacre. Among them were barons and nobles who had hoped by these means to escape repayment of what they owed. But in this they were mistaken as there were copies of their debts in other places. For years after, the Exchequer collected the debts, which, owing to the death of the Jews of York, became the property of the king.

To this day one of Rabbi Yomtov's hymns is chanted in synagogue on Kol Nidrei night, the eve of the Day of Atonement.

THE EXCHEQUER OF THE JEWS

Richard left England in 1190 for the Crusades and remained in the East for some two years. It is related that there he offered the post of royal physician to the famous rabbi and philosopher, Moses Maimonides, who was also a noted physician. But Maimonides declined this honour preferring to remain in the service of the Mohammedan ruler of Egypt.

We all know the story of Richard's capture and imprisonment on his way homeward, how for some time nothing was known of his whereabouts or fate until he was traced by Blondin his faithful minstrel. His captor, the Duke of Austria, demanded a huge ransom for his release. This money was collected throughout the length and breadth of England. As usual, Jews were forced to pay a sum totally out of proportion to their numbers.

In 1194 Richard returned to England. In need of money, he ordered an enquiry into the Jewish position. It must be remembered that all the property of the Jews was regarded by the king as his own. Therefore when the records of the debts due to Jews were lost during the riots after Richard's coronation, it was the royal treasury that suffered.

Richard resolved that this should not happen again. The enquiry was for the purpose of finding out what property was owned by the Jews who had been massacred, and the manner in which the Jewish bankers carried on their business and kept their records.

Hubert Walter, Archbishop of Canterbury, was in charge of the royal enquiry. The plan which he prepared for safeguarding the royal treasury was indeed ingenious. It was ordered that all records of business dealings by Jews should be registered, and special offices were set up for this purpose. Records of all their business were to be kept in two copies. One copy was kept by the Jewish bankers who made the loan, while the other was put into a special wooden chest which was to be found in every city where Jews dwelt. These chests, sometimes called archa, served the same purpose as the safes in banks in modern times.

Every chest or archa, was stoutly built. It was bound with iron and had three locks and three keys. Five officials were in charge of each chest. Of these two were Jews and the other three were Christians. Two of them fulfilled the same duties as the two Jews and like them were called

chirographers. The fifth man was an official of
the royal treasury. The Jewish chirographers kept
one key, the Christian chirographers another,
while the third was held by the treasury official
who represented the king. This was done to prevent any one person opening the chest except in
the presence of the others. By this means fraud
and forgery by any one party was made
impossible.

The chirographs, or documents, were written
on one sheet of parchment and afterwards
divided. An account of these was kept on a roll.
They were cut in an irregular zig-zag fashion so
that when repayment was made the cut parts
fitted like a jig-saw puzzle. This was to prevent
false chirographs being used.

Every registry office had an archa. Later, Jews
were allowed to reside only in towns where there
were these chests. Altogether twenty-seven of
these chests existed, in different parts of the
country.

As a result, whatever happened to the Jews,
their business records were preserved and the
king's Exchequer could suffer no loss. Whenever
needed, the chest, sealed and locked, could be sent
to London to be inspected at the Exchequer.

The records were for the most part written in
Latin, but the receipts for repayment were written
in Hebrew. These were mostly with a Latin trans-

lation. Sometimes they were translated into Norman-French and at times in Latin written in Hebrew characters. These receipts were called by their Hebrew name of *Shetar*.

From these offices where the chests were kept, and out of that branch of the Exchequer which had had the control of Aaron of Lincoln's estate since his death in 1186 (see page 52) a separate department of the treasury came into being. This was called the Exchequer of the Jews.

In 1198 four men were selected from among the Barons of the Exchequer to be justices or wardens of the Jews. They were in charge of the Exchequer of the Jews. Any disputes between Jews and Christians were tried by them. Jews giving evidence before the justices would take an oath, holding the Scrolls of the Law in their arms. Sometimes, in the case of a dispute between Jews, the assistance of learned Jews was sought on questions regarding Jewish law. In the course of time the Exchequer of the Jews came to deal with all matters concerning the Jewish community. A Jewish representative called the Chief Presbyter was appointed. His position was similar to that of a Chief Rabbi of the Jews in England today.

These orderly arrangements replaced the earlier conditions. Till then the records of Jewish dealings were scattered among the different Pipe

Rolls (see page 40). But from now on they were brought together under the special department in London which was in charge of all the chests throughout the kingdom.

So well were these records guarded and preserved that they exist to this day in the Public Record Office in London.

It is from them that learned men have been able to piece together most of what is known to us of the history of the Jews in Medieval England.

Apart from chirographs, rent-rolls and pledges, which were kept in the chests, there were also tallies. From the illustration facing p. 48 you will see what a tally looked like. It was made of a narrow strip of wood from nine to twelve inches in length. Notches were cut along the lower and upper edges, differing in shape and size according to the amount of money the tally was to represent. On each side of the wood an inscription was written, giving particulars of the tally. Tallies were used as receipts for payment in either money or goods.

Now, just as chirographs were cut in two, so that forgery should be impossible, tallies were split into two unequal lengths. One part was retained by the seller or creditor, the other by the debtor. If there was any dispute both parts of the tally had to be produced, to see if they 'tallied' or fitted.

In those far-off days, this was such a convenient and popular form for business purposes, that the royal exchequer gave tallies as official receipts. English Jews being so prominent in the business world made extensive use of tallies and several of these with Hebrew inscriptions have been preserved.

KING JOHN 1199–1216

When John ascended the throne in 1199, the Exchequer of the Jews was in full running order. By sending out notices to the different towns where chests were deposited, the king could order these to be specially sealed and sent to London to be inspected at the Exchequer. Thus he would know exactly the wealth of his Jews.

As a result of the disorders of Richard's reign the condition of the Jews was no longer as good as formerly and many had returned to the Continent. Of those who remained much of their wealth was diminished. John saw the need for protecting Jews against both the onslaughts of his unruly subjects and the greed of the Exchequer. He was wise enough to understand that it would be like killing the goose that laid the golden eggs to ill-treat and tax the Jews too much. In the first years of his reign John began a charter with the words, 'The king to all his faithful, *both to all the Jews and English,* greeting...'

He appointed Jacob of London as chief presbyter of the Jews, the first to hold the office. He granted him complete freedom of movement

71

throughout the land, calling him 'our Royal Jew'. In the safe conduct, which was a kind of passport for travelling all over the country, he was described by John as 'our well beloved friend'. He also ordered that all public notices to Jews should be announced in the synagogues. Leo the Jew was John's own goldsmith and jeweller.

In 1201 John granted a charter of liberties to all the Jews of Normandy and England. In this charter the king directed that Jews and their possessions were to be protected.

Disputes between Jews were to be settled in the Jewish court of law, the Beth Din. Jews could again move freely throughout the land, could buy and sell without hindrance. To have this charter confirmed cost the Jews 4,000 marks – a very large sum in those days. (At that time the mark was used for accounts, but not for buying things in shops.)

But though the king knew the value of his Jews both for the filling of his own purse and the commerce of his country, the people did not. In 1204, there were some attacks against them in London. They appealed to John for protection and he at once wrote to the mayor and barons of London. He declared that he was amazed that knowing the protection he had granted the Jews, they had suffered them to be badly treated. He further ordered that they were to take particular care for the future declaring, 'If any ill happened to the Jews through their connivance or neglect, they should be answerable for it.'

For some years Jews enjoyed fair conditions, John treating them with justice as set forth in his charter. In 1206 John lost Normandy and with it a great deal of wealth. From that time his attitude to the Jews changed completely. The promises and the charter given at the beginning of his reign were forgotten. Persecution began anew.

For the Jews the loss of Normandy was a serious blow. Since the days of their settlement under William the Conqueror, they had been in constant touch with their brethren across the Channel. Apart from being under the same king, they spoke the same language and their interests were the same. They were now cut off from the Jewish centres in Europe. The great scholars and rabbis of the Continent who, till then, had visited the Angevin Jewish communities, could no longer come as formerly: England had once again become separated from Europe – and the Jews of England were cut off from their brethren on the Continent.

It was John's efforts to recapture Normandy, his costly and unsuccessful wars against Wales and his own barons that was the cause of his change of policy towards our ancestors. It began with the confiscation of Jewish property. The knights who accompanied him and fought in the wars, were released from their debts to Jews. The chests of the Jews were examined, the exact state of their possessions discovered and a heavy tax of 66,000 marks, a sum well over £1,250,000 in modern money levied on them. In 1210, all the Jews were cast into prison until this sum was paid.

Jews were tortured to reveal where their money was hidden to force them to quicker payment. Terrible means were used to force money from them. It is related that one Jew of Bristol was fined an excessive sum and as he refused to pay this unjust demand a tooth was pulled out of his jaw every day. He bore the terrible pain for seven days. On the eighth day he could stand it no longer; perhaps his friends had managed to collect the fine. In any case on the eighth day the fine was paid. Other Jews had their eyes plucked out. We must remember that these were the Dark Ages, when every prison was a dungeon and tortures by means of hot irons and other instruments were used on unlucky prisoners. The poorer Jews who could not pay the tax demanded had to flee the country. So desperate was their condition that one of the old chroniclers relates that many Jewish men and women were reduced to such poverty that they 'begged from door to door and prowled about the city like dogs'.

There was an exodus of Jews from England. So great was the number who left, that one writer states that in this year there was an expulsion of Jews from the kingdom. But though harried and robbed at every turn, Jews did not forget their origin. More than ever they turned their eyes in longing to their ancient homeland. In 1211 Rabbi Joseph ben Baruk of Colchester summoned a meeting in London to persuade Jews of Angevin England to go with him to Palestine. We know that about this time three hundred French and English rabbis set out on a pilgrimage to the Land of Israel, then alas, barren and a waste under the rule of strangers.

For some four years John did not molest the Jews and they were able to carry on their usual activities. Then, again money was demanded and many were cast into prison. About this time the barons revolted and took up arms against the king. Between the greed of the king and the violence of the barons, Jews were indeed in a sorry plight. Their houses were seized and given to royal favourites. When the barons occupied London in 1215, the Jewish quarter, called the Jewry, was the first district plundered. Houses and buildings were demolished and their stones used for strengthening the walls of the city against the onslaught of the royal troops. In 1586, more than 350 years later, when Ludgate, one of the gates of London, was repaired, a large stone was uncovered. It bore a Hebrew inscription, and proved to be the tombstone of 'Rabbi Moses the son of the learned and wise Rabbi Isaac'. It is thought that this memorial stone was taken away by the barons from the Jewish cemetery. Up to the year 1177 the only Jewish cemetery was situated in London; and from all over the kingdom Jews were laid to rest here.

Magna Carta, for which king John is chiefly remembered in history, also refers to the English Jews of that period. But unlike the rest of this great charter, it dealt only with the wealth of the Jews and was of profit only to the barons. It gave the Jews no rights whatsoever.

HENRY III 1216–1272

Henry III came to the throne at the age of nine. The kingdom was ruled during his childhood by the wise Earl of Pembroke who acted as regent. The Earl restored peace and order after the unrest of John's reign and set free all Jews who were then in prison. In 1217, when preparations were being made for a Crusade proclaimed two years earlier by the Pope, strict orders were sent to the sheriffs of every city where there were Jews. They were commanded to protect all Jews in their cities and to see that they came to no harm, especially at the hands of the Crusaders. Once again Jews from the Continent were encouraged to come and settle in England. On the other hand, those wishing leave to depart from England were allowed to do so only by special licence. This shows that they were highly valued by the regent who did not wish to lose the services they rendered.

At this period the Church was very powerful. Laws against the Jews which had been passed by a Council of the Church in 1215 were now put into force in England. For the first time English Jews had to wear a special badge on their outer garments. The badge was white or light yellow in colour. It was shaped like the two tablets of stone bearing the Ten Commandments which you

sometimes see over the holy Ark in the synagogue, a symbol of the tablets which Moses brought down from Mount Sinai. This special badge marked out the Jews as distinct and separate from the rest of the population.

Despite the Church Laws, the regent continued to treat Jews fairly. Once again the Jews of England felt at ease. They were happy to forget the past ill-treatment and the sad days that had gone. The regent kept loyal watch over them and when the Church strove to interfere with their rights, he came to their aid.

Left at peace, many Jews became prosperous, and the records tell us a great deal about some of them. The most important Jew of this period was the famous Isaac of Norwich who could be described as the Rothschild of those days. We know that Isaac of Norwich owned property in many parts of the country as well as many ships and a quay at Norwich. But in the past his wealth had not saved him from imprisonment. When King John arrested all the Jews of England in 1210 (see page 74), Isaac was taken to the Tower of London. The fine house he owned in London was seized by the king and given to the Earl of Derby. Isaac died in 1247.

But prosperity and peace were, however, short-lived. The king came of age in 1227. The regents – the Earl of Pembroke had been followed by Hubert de Burgh – ceased to rule and a change was soon noticed in the treatment of the Jews. Fines were levied. Time after time the king forced Jews to pay great sums into the Royal treasury.

The Church became even more jealous of the Jews in its fear of their influence, especially in matters of religion. About this time a certain deacon of the Church embraced the Jewish faith. He was burnt at the stake at Oxford for becoming a Jew.

Up to this time Jews had been allowed to practise their religion freely. As we have seen, Jewish learning and the Hebrew language flourished despite hardship. Under the rule of the two good regents, the Earl of Pembroke and Hubert de Burgh, the Jews of London had built a stately synagogue. Its beauty now roused the envy of certain monks. On their petition this house of worship was seized by the king and given to the monks of the Order of St Anthony for their use as a church.

From this time onward, with scarcely a change, the history of the Jews of medieval England is one long story of taxation, persecution and ill-treatment. On public holidays, or whenever there was an occasion for public festivity, Jews went in fear of their lives. When the king celebrated his marriage to Eleanor of Provence, all London Jews took refuge in the Tower, for they remembered what had happened on the coronation day of Richard I.

In 1231 conditions took a still worse turn when Simon de Montfort, brother-in-law of the king, drove the Jews from the city of Leicester which was his property. This example was followed by other cities. In 1234 they were driven from Newcastle; in 1235 from Wycombe; in 1236 from Southampton; from Berkhamsted in 1242; in 1244 from Newbury. Moreover, in order to prevent the Jews from moving into other cities, it was decreed in 1253 that Jews could live only in the cities in which they resided at that date. But this did not give them security, for in 1263, they were driven also from Derby.

F

THE DOMUS CONVERSORUM

On the site of the present Public Record Office in Chancery Lane, London, there stood in former years a building called by the Latin name of Domus Conversorum, which in English means House of the Converts. This was erected by king Henry III, in 1232, as a home for those Jews who were converted from Judaism to Christianity. Henry built the Domus for the ransom of his own soul, as well as that of his father, King John; in fact, for the sake of the souls of all their ancestors.

The Domus Conversorum was the king's gift or endowment. A house of a wealthy Jew which had come into the king's hands was used for this purpose, as well as the land surrounding it. The converts who dwelt in this house were provided not only with their lodging but with clothing and money. Having their safety, lodging and sustenance secured, strong indeed was the temptation for Jews to convert in those times.

Deep interest was taken by the Church in the Domus. It was hoped by providing safety and favoured treatment, to entice all Jews from their ancient faith. What wonder then that some Jews, less strong to resist persecution, were tempted to seek conversion? Members of the royal family acted as the godparents of the converts when they were baptized.

The Domus stood in Chancery Lane until 1837, when the present Public Record Office was erected in its place. Here in time the treasury records, or rolls were kept in the custody of the Keeper, later called the Master of the Rolls.

In 1241 representatives of all the twenty-one Jewish communities were ordered by the king to appear in Worcester to be present at a so-called Parliament of the Jews. The larger communities were each to send six representatives, the smaller two. These were to meet in the words of the royal order, to 'treat with the king as well concerning his own as their advantage'. With the hope in their hearts that their burden was to be lifted, and that they would be able to discuss their position fully and frankly, the Jews set off for Worcester. But alas for their hopes! They found they had been summoned to arrange among themselves a tax of 20,000 marks.

Aghast at the vastness of the sum, they protested and as their words of protest seemed to fall on deaf ears, they sent spokesmen to the Court in London. But the king, too, was deaf to their pleas and ordered that the money be promptly paid. Many Jews unable to pay their portion of the tallage or taxation were arrested together with their wives and children and imprisoned in the Tower, their property being seized in payment of their fine.

Henry, despite his religious views and pretence of piety, in 1244 again imposed a fine on the Jews. This time, on the pretext that they had committed a ritual murder, he demanded 60,000 marks. Six years passed before this sum could be collected. On one occasion, so fearful were the Jews of a repetition of their savage imprisonment, that they sent their wives and children into hiding. It seemed clear that the king was resolved to rob them of all their possessions.

Once more, in 1250, the king was in need of money and sought to squeeze it from the Jews. He asked his brother, Earl Richard, to collect the sum. But this time the Jews made a stand. The leading Jews with the Chief Presbyter Elias at their head, went to plead with Earl Richard. They had made up their minds to request that either these numerous taxes should be dropped, or that they should be permitted to leave the country. 'We entreat, for God's sake,' said Rabbi Elias to Earl Richard, 'that he (the king) would give us license and safe conduct of departing out of his kingdom, that we may seek and find . . .

some other place, under some prince who bears some bowels of mercy, and some stability of truth and faithfulness. And we will depart, never to return again, leaving here our household stuff and houses behind us . . . He hath people, yea his own merchants, I say not usurers who by usurous contracts, heap up infinite sums of money. Let the king rely upon them and seek after their profits. Verily they have supplanted us and made us poor. Which the king, however, pretends not to know, exacting from us those things we cannot give him, although he would pull out our eye, or cut our throats, when he had first pulled off our skins.'

Earl Richard declared that their request to leave the country could not be granted, for the king of France had issued an order against his Jews, and where else could they go? Henry, he added, would for the present accept as much money as they could give.

The following year the king again tried to raise large sums from the Jews. But he failed, for their wealth had already been taken from them. Thereupon the king, who as has been explained, treated the Jews as his personal property, sold them for some years to his brother, Earl Richard for the sum of £5,000. This meant that Earl Richard was free to tax the Jews for that period and make a profit on the sum he had paid to the king. He was, however, lenient to them. Under his care conditions improved.

At the end of this period the Jews were sold for a further term of three years to prince Edward, the king's son. After a year Edward sold them to a company of Christian usurers, known as Cahorsin, who were Italians in the service of the Pope; their rates of interest were higher than the Jewish rate. The Chief Presbyter, Rabbi Elias, had referred to the Cahorsin when he reminded the king that if the Jews were allowed to depart, he would still have his own Christian money-lenders for enriching his treasury.

LITTLE ST HUGH OF LINCOLN – 1255

You will remember the first accusation of ritual murder, that of William of Norwich in 1144 (p. 43): the false charge which had cost so many innocent lives. Up to 1255 there had been other such false charges. But in 1255 occurred the best known of all the false accusations, that of the boy known as Little St Hugh of Lincoln.

It so happened that at this time a large party of Jews from different parts of the country were gathered in Lincoln. They had come to be present at the wedding of Belaset, daughter of Magister Benedict, son of Moses. He is better known as Berachiah ben Moses, a well known Rabbinical scholar and Hebrew writer of that time.

The bailiff of the city was informed of the discovery of a little boy's body in the well of a Jew named Copin – and immediately the cry arose that the Jews were responsible for his death. Copin, while the wedding party was still assembled, was seized and threatened with death if he did not confess. Terrified for his own safety and unable to endure the tortures he had to suffer, a 'confession' was forced from him. He said that every year Jews crucify a boy in mockery of Jesus. Even the monkish chronicler who relates this story called Copin's confession 'ravings'.

The boy, Hugh by name, was immediately made a martyr and saint. The king, who happened at that time to be in the neighbourhood, hurried to Lincoln to enquire into the matter. Here was a chance not to be missed of filling his own coffers with money he could demand in fines and by seizing the property of Jews! He ordered Copin to be tied to a horse's tail and dragged through the hilly streets and afterwards hanged.

About one hundred Jews were arrested and brought to London, to appear for trial. Some eighteen demanded their rights to appear before a jury consisting half of Jews, for well they knew what little justice they could expect at the hands of a Christian jury inflamed by popular prejudice. Without trial, without a hearing, these men were hanged. The rest were tried, declared guilty and sentenced to death. But before they could be hanged, some Franciscan and Dominican monks, who were well aware that the charge against them was false, appealed on their behalf to the king. They had the support of the king's brother, Richard of Cornwall. The appeals were successful and the innocent men were released.

The splendid shrine erected to the boy Hugh in Lincoln Cathedral became a place of pilgrimage. Numerous ballads were written about him in French and English; and Geoffrey Chaucer in the *Canterbury Tales* tells of ritual murder in the Nun's tale. Thus, for centuries, the story of the boy saint was a popular folk tale throughout the land. People who had never seen a Jew knew of Jews only through these horrible and lying ballads.

It is therefore pleasing to add, even though seven hundred years later, that the falsity of the story of 'Little Saint Hugh' has now been publicly proclaimed for all to read in the very same cathedral in which so many pilgrims came to his shrine. The shrine itself was destroyed by Oliver Cromwell's soldiers, but a notice was hung where it had been, and repeated the lying tale.

Since 1959 this notice has been removed and in its place another notice placed by the Dean of Lincoln Cathedral declares stories of ritual murders of Christian boys by Jewish communities to be 'trumped up' charges . . . 'and fictions which have cost innocent Jewish lives . . .' The notice ends: 'Such stories do not redound to the credit of Christendom, and we pray "Remember not, Lord, our offences nor the offences of our forefathers".'

CIVIL WAR

The struggle between the barons and the king meant further suffering for the Jews. Simon de Montfort, the leader of the barons, had already shown his hatred for Jews by driving them from Leicester. They hated the Jews because it was by the aid of the money extracted from them by the king that he was able to fight the barons. Whenever the barons captured a city, they made

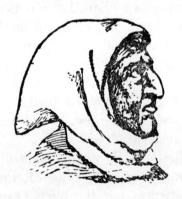

straight for the registry where the chest or archa of the Jews was kept, broke off the locks and trampled the proofs of debts underfoot, afterwards setting fire to what remained.

The Civil War was heralded with a massacre of London Jews in 1262, when about 700 Jews were slain. The barons entered London and the king himself took refuge in the Tower. The city was left without protection and the mob took the opportunity to search the Jewish quarter and murder many of the inhabitants.

This was followed by similar massacres in the following year in Winchester, Worcester, and again in 1263, in London, Lincoln, Canterbury and Bristol, and, in fact, in almost every town where Jews lived. Jewish property was pillaged, Jewish records destroyed. Jewish blood flowed freely. On the Continent, Jews mourned their martyred brethren in England and for many years afterwards recited prayers in their memory on the sad anniversary.

In 1264 further disorders broke out and many Jews fled overseas. The struggle between the king and barons was long and bitter as we know from our English history. When in February, 1266, the London Jews were again forced to seek refuge in the Tower, they joined in its defence. Ancient records tell us that they manned the ramparts of the Tower against de Montfort's army.

In 1264 Simon de Montfort was victorious, and the Jews of England expected no mercy. Nevertheless, as soon as he was in power, he realised the value of the Jews to the country, and took steps to put a stop to the attacks on them. Those who had taken refuge in the Tower of London and certain castles throughout the country returned to their homes under his promise of protection. De Montfort remained in power for nearly two years. In 1265, king Henry III was again supreme. Once more there was a change in the

treatment of the Jews. New laws were passed which made it impossible for them to hold land or to carry on their ordinary business. So poor did they become that in 1271 they were unable to pay a tax of 6,000 marks. When a further fine of 5,000 marks was levied, all who could not pay their share were imprisoned. Even the

Cahorsin, the Christian usurers who were the business rivals of the Jews, pitied their lot. A chronicler of the period relates that 'nothing but weeping and wailing was to be seen in every corner'.

When Henry III died in 1272 after a long reign of fifty-six years the Jews in England had been reduced from prosperity to a state of abject poverty.

It is pleasant to relate, however, that in this troubled period many English Christians remained friendly with the Jews, visiting their houses and even attending the synagogues. They also took part in recreations and sport together. We know of one occasion when they joined with their Christian neighbours in chasing the deer. This was an unlawful act for any except the king and his lords.

It chanced that on 7th December, in the year 1277, certain men of Colchester, in the county of Essex, seeing a doe running from a wood on the outskirts of the city, across the streets, ran in pursuit of the deer. Leading the chase was Saunte, son of Ursel, Cok and Samuel, sons of Aaron, Isaac the Jewish chaplain, Copin and Elias, as well as certain Christians. 'And these with a mighty clamour chased the same doe, and so worried her by their shouting, that they forced her to jump a wall and she thus broke her neck,' relates the account.

There was a hue and cry at this destruction of royal game. These Colchester men were ordered to be brought before the justices. Saunte and Isaac were convicted and thrown into prison. The others, Jews and Christians, alike, were fined certain sums.

The clerk of the justices who wrote the report of this case on parchment in the year 1277, amused himself in an unusual way. He sketched a kind of cartoon of a Jew of the period in the margin of the report. Above it, he wrote 'Aaron, son of the Devil'. In this, one of the earliest drawings of a Jew, we see him wearing the costume and peaked cowl of the period which showed he was not an outdoor worker or labourer. On his breast is the Jewish badge, two tablets in shape, which all Jews were forced to wear. (See illustration on page 93)

EDWARD I AND EXPULSION 1272–1290

When Edward I came to the throne just over two hundred years had passed since William of Normandy conquered England. During that period the Jews of England had lived through times that were happy and times that were unhappy. For the most part it was a period of great suffering and constant danger. The day was now approaching when, like their ancestors the Israelites in Egypt, they would have to pack the few belongings which they could carry with them and depart out of the kingdom.

When Henry III died the new king, Edward I, was abroad, fighting in the crusades. Two years passed before he came back to England to take his place on the throne. During that time a heavy tax was once again imposed on the Jews, so heavy that they were unable to pay it. At the same time the Church took a hand in further depriving the Jews of their livelihood by preaching against their being allowed to carry on their business of banking. Now, although the Church preached against these pursuits on the ground that they were against the law of the Christian religion, they

The petition of 1656 signed by Menasseh ben Israel and others.
Counter-signature of Oliver Cromwell in bottom left-hand corner

Chief Rabbi Solomon Hirschell. A contemporary print (1808).

allowed, as we have seen, the Cahorsin, their own Christian usurers, to follow the business of money-lending. Indeed, the Popes themselves lent money on usury and thus broke their own laws.

And thus, having been robbed, heavily taxed and frequently massacred for two centuries, the Jews of England were now too poor to be of further service to the king.

So Edward I turned to another plan. He decided to provide them with other means of livelihood. A law was passed by Parliament in 1275 called the Law Concerning the Jews.

Hitherto, the Jews had been kept to one main pursuit, that of money-lending or banking. There were, indeed, numbers of Jews who were engaged in various crafts and employments, some being physicians with their own herbarium, or garden of herbs for use as medicines to cure illnesses. Abraham Balistarius, though a Jew, was a cross-bowman, while Abraham le Peysoner followed the trade of a fishmonger as his name indicates. Others were goldsmiths, wine and wool merchants, cheesemongers – as well as dealers in other merchandise. They could not, however, be-long to the trade guilds which were confined to Christians, and which controlled all the industries in the country. The result was that only a few Jews were to be found in industry. They were not allowed to own land for farming, so that this,

G

the chief employment in England at that time, was also closed to them. The Law Concerning the Jews at one stroke, stopped the Jews from

following the practice of banking or money-lending their main occupation. It even prevented them from collecting the profits of money already lent by them. On the other hand, the Law seemed to open up other pursuits. It permitted them to become merchants and artisans to rent land for farming for a period of up to fifteen years and travel more freely about the country.

As the Law Concerning the Jews meant that they would now mix more with the general population than formerly and friendship between Jews and Christians would increase, the Church again stepped in. King Edward was warned by the Church against the danger of Jews mixing freely with Christians, as would happen if Jews spread throughout the country to follow the pursuits now permitted to them. The Church greatly feared religious discussion between Jews and Christians and the likelihood of Christians being drawn to the Jewish faith. So as to separate them even more, the regulation of the Jew badge, worn only by Jewish men, was made stricter. It was now ordered that all Jews and Jewesses from the age of seven should not fail to wear the Jew Badge, and that the colour should be yellow, and thus more noticeable than the former white badge which quickly became discoloured and could not be so easily noticed.

As was to be expected, the Law Concerning the Jews failed to provide new means of livelihood. Representatives of all the Jewish communities in England met and drew up a petition to the king pointing out that as they could not travel in safety permission to travel was of no value. They were not allowed to belong to the guilds which, as has been explained, controlled all the trades, and so they would have to pay higher prices for the goods they bought and would be forced to sell more dearly than Christian merchants.

Very soon, in 1275, although trade and all the former Jewish business had been made impossible for them, a heavy tax was again imposed. Many unable to pay their portion were imprisoned and their wives and children sent out of the country. This was repeated several times, but it was now quite clear that little more could be squeezed from the Jews of England.

They were faced with utter ruin. In despair, several gave up their Jewish faith and entered the Domus Conversorum, or House of the Converts. Others escaped out of England, fearing that the king, enraged by the failure to force more money out of them, would devise some new persecution, especially as his Queen Eleanor and his mother, Queen Eleanor of Provence, were both known to be haters of Jews.

And how tragically were the Jewish fears fulfilled!

The king needed much money for he lived in great luxury. His silver plate and the gold and jewels of his court were famous. Time and again he had need of larger and larger sums of money which he could no longer get from the Jews. In 1278 he ordered the arrest of all the Jews of England on a charge of 'clipping the coin of the realm'.

Look at any silver coin. You will see that it is notched at regular intervals along the edge. This is called a milled edge. In early days coins had no milled edges, so that the edge wore unevenly, and when thin would even snap. Dishonest people took advantage of this by 'clipping' or filing off small quantities of the silver from each coin. They would then melt down the scraps which they would sell at a good profit. This was a common crime and severely punished, sometimes even with death. There had been occasions when Jewish, as well as Christian merchants had been accused of clipping coins. Although there had been a number of enquiries it was never found that the practice was more common to Jews than to others.

But in 1278, Jews as a whole were suddenly accused of the practice. All the Jews of the realm were arrested. Many were sent in chains for trial in London, and thrown into the Tower. Two hundred and sixty Jews were hanged for coin-clipping, their property being seized by the king. Among them were many prominent men and women who would not have stooped to such an act. Gentiles who had been arrested on the same charge were released on the payment of fines.

There can be no doubt that the charge of coin-clipping was simply an excuse for robbing the Jews of the little they still owned, for the property of the Jews who were hanged passed by law into the hands of the king. Years afterwards when there were no longer any Jewish merchants in England, coin-clipping was as rife as ever, and it was necessary for Parliament to pass new laws against it.

Not satisfied with taking away their possessions, the king also sought to get them to give up what was much more precious, their Jewish faith. He wrote to the sheriffs of the cities ordering them to force all Jews to be present at services where Dominican priests would preach Christian sermons.

THE EXPULSION – 1290

By now the king decided that nothing more could be squeezed from the Jews.

Again in 1279 the false accusation of Ritual Murder was raised by the king, and Jews were dragged in chains through the streets, many dying as a result of this cruel treatment. Charges of selling the metal of coin-clippings were once more brought against them. In 1287, all the Jews were thrown into prison and not released until a fine of 20,000 marks had been paid, reducing the whole community to a state of utter poverty. Queen Eleanor, mother of the king, encouraged him in all his anti-Jewish measures. She herself, though she employed a Jew to manage her own business affairs, had expelled Jews from the towns which belonged to her, such as Gloucester, Worcester and Cambridge, where they had been long settled.

The Law Concerning the Jews was a failure. The Church Council met and passed new restrictions against the Jews even forbidding them to practice medicine. Edward, urged by his consort, Queen Eleanor of Provence, bowing as always to

103

the wish of the Church, in 1287 expelled the Jews from his estates in Gascony, in France.

The news of this made Edward popular in England and on his return Parliament promised him a part of the Jewish possessions and the Church another part if he would expel the English Jews from his kingdom. Business jealousy, dislike of aliens, religious prejudices and incitements of evil men all worked together to bring about the doom of the Jews in England.

Edward proved a willing tool. On 18th July 1290, the decree of expulsion was signed by the king. By a strange and sad turn of fate it fell on the fast of the ninth of Ab. This most tragic day in our Hebrew calendar is the anniversary of the destruction of both Temples in Jerusalem. A bitter memory for all Jews, it was doubly bitter for those early English Jews who, after generations of settlement in England, were to be cast out.

The decree ordered all Jews to leave England on the feast of All Saints, which fell that year on November 1st. Throughout the country, by Royal proclamation people were commanded in the interval not to 'injure, damage or grieve' the Jews! The poorest Jews were to travel at cheap rates; and all were allowed to take with them their money and movables. But their bonds and lands, which included the synagogues, school houses and cemetries were confiscated by the king. Some specially favoured Jews, such as Cok, son of Hagin, who was in the Queen's service, were allowed to sell their houses and debts.

On Tuesday October 10th, 1290, began the exodus of the Jews, in all 15,066, from England. On that day, the poorer Jews of London started out for the coast, bearing before them the Holy Scrolls of the Law. Most of the wealthier Jews embarked at London, taking what possessions they could with them.

It is related that at Queenborough, at the mouth of the Thames, one of the ships grounded on the sands at ebb-tide. The master of the ship cast anchor and invited his passengers to walk on the shore, until the tide was high enough for the ship to float. He led them some distance, then when the tide began to rise, rushed into the water, and by means of a rope swung himself on deck. Turning to the stranded Jews on the shore, he cried mockingly that if they needed help they should call on Moses who led their ancestors the Israelites through the Red Sea on their departure from Egypt. All the Jews were drowned and the sailors divided their few pitiful belongings amongst themselves. But justice was meted out in this case at least, for afterwards the master and his accomplices were charged with murder and hanged.

Some of the expelled Jews set sail for France. It was then early winter, a season notorious for stormy seas in the English Channel. At this time, fierce tempests raged. Many Jews were drowned. Others were cast on shore. All their poor possessions lost in the sea, they were destitute and at the mercy of the French king, who despite the Pope's protests allowed them to settle for a time in Amiens.

Some of the exiles settled in Paris, others joined their brethren who lived in Spain. Yet others travelled further afield, and wherever there was a Jewish community, no matter how far away and scattered, there they found a haven.

PART II
THE MIDDLE PERIOD
From the Expulsion to Manasseh ben Israel
1290–1664

THE MIDDLE PERIOD 1290–1664

The next period in the history of the Jews of England, the Middle Period, is so named because it comes between the year of the Expulsion, which occurred in 1290, and the year 1664, when Jews were allowed the protection of the English law and the right to live openly as Jews in England.

The Middle Period covers a most important time in the history of England. During the span of 374 years there occurred a number of outstanding events which affected the whole future of the human race. It was also a period of striking progress in literature and science. The great events were as follows:

1. The Renaissance or the spreading of a knowledge of science and ancient literature and art which had first appeared in Italy, had flowered in England by the sixteenth century.

2. The Reformation.

3. The Discovery of America in 1492.

In all these events Jews played a part. The progress of England like that of other countries was therefore in a measure due to Jews.

The Renaissance was the rebirth of learning,

and among its scholars were many Jews. Indeed, the Jews played a very great part in the translating of the works of science and literature into the languages of Europe. One result was that the

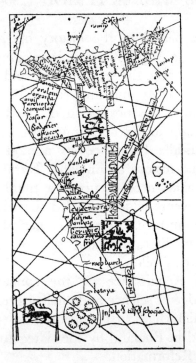

Hebrew language became more widely known and Jews were in great demand for teaching Hebrew to Christians. The more complete knowledge of the Bible which this brought about greatly helped forward the Reformation. This

was an attempt by men to free themselves from the authority of the Church and enable them to have their own opinions on religion.

Also, in the discovery of America, Jews played a prominent part. Indeed, it is now believed by many historians that Columbus himself came from a Jewish family that had been forced into conversion to Christianity in Spain and had later settled in Genoa. These forced converts frequently continued to practise the Jewish faith in secret. Such secret Jews were called Marranos. You will come across this name very often in the later history of English Jews. Together with Columbus there were a number of Marranos on the very ship from which the New World was first sighted. The first man to sight the American shore on Columbus' ship was Rodrigo de Triano, a Marrano. The first man to step on the soil of the New World was Luis de Torres, another Marrano. The maps used by Columbus were drawn by Jewish map-makers; for the Jewish cartographers or map-makers of those days were widely celebrated for their skill, and their maps were most frequently used by sea voyagers.

The discovery of America opened up a great new world and provided men and women from Europe with new lands for settlement.

During the Middle Period there also occurred a number of disasters in Jewish history, the effects of which you will come across in later chapters. It is important that they should be borne in mind. They are: the Expulsion of the Jews from Spain in 1492, and the terrible massacres of the Jews of Eastern Europe in the year 1648. Both these events scattered vast numbers of Jewish refugees throughout the known world, forcing them to seek new homes.

Such are the chief features of the Middle Period.

Lord George Gordon

The Great Synagogue, Dukes Place, in 1808 (after Rowlandson)

AFTER THE EXPULSION

The Expulsion in 1290 did not result in all the Jews leaving England. A number remained behind living either as converts in the House of Converts in London, or dwelling secretly in remote towns and villages.

The possessions left behind by those who were expelled became the property of the king who, writes John Stow, the 16th century historian, 'made of them a mightie masse of money'. He presented some of the fine houses to his favourites.

But Jews did not cease to come to England. From time to time refugees made their way to this country and entered the House of Converts. One of these converts, Sir Edward Brampton, played an important part in English history. He was a soldier from Portugal who came to England and entered the House of Converts. Edward IV acted as godfather at his baptism. He fought gallantly in the Wars of the Roses and was knighted for his services in 1483. When his side, the Yorkist, was defeated, he returned to Portugal, taking with him, in his service, a certain Flemish youth, Perkin Warbeck by name. It was from Sir Edward Brampton that Warbeck learnt all the details concerning life at the court of Edward IV. This knowledge Perkin afterwards used when he made his unsuccessful claim to the throne posing as Richard, Duke of York, one of the two princes who had been murdered in the Tower.

From time to time Jews came openly to England either as physicians or on special missions, at the invitation of kings and nobles. In 1409 Dick Whittington, the famous Lord Mayor of London, brought a Jewish physician, Master Samson de Mirabeau, from the Continent to attend his wife Lady Alice. From as far distant a land as Italy, King Henry IV summoned Elias Sabot, a Jewish doctor who brought with him ten men of his faith to make up a *minyan,* the smallest number required for Jewish public worship. In 1318 a Jew named Isaac came from the Holy Land to collect the ransom of a Knight Hospitaller. The knight had been captured in one of the Crusades and was allowed to accompany Isaac to England where the ransom was to be paid. Also, among the Lombard merchants who had replaced the Jews as bankers, there were believed to be a number of Jews; for in 1378 a complaint was made in Parliament that Jews were in England in the guise of Lombard merchants.

Of the actual names of Jews in England during the early part of the Middle Period, we know only those who came to public notice and are thus mentioned in the records that still exist. There were many more whose names are unknown. For example, in 1498 when the Prince of Wales, son of Henry VII was betrothed to Catherine of Aragon, her parents, the king and queen of Spain, tried to get Henry VII to refuse haven to Marranos, the secret Jews of Spain, many of whom had succeeded in escaping to England.

By the time Henry VIII came to the throne, there was a small Jewish community both in London and Bristol several of whom were physicians who were living as Marranos – 'the exiles of Portugal who have their homes in England' they are described by a 16th century Jewish writer. From the port of Bristol sailed ships carrying the early adventurers to the New World, planters and traders who laid the foundations of the great republics beyond the sea. Among them were many Marranos who made Bristol a port of call, frequently staying on for a time and adding to the small Jewish community. Sometimes they passed on to London where there was also a secret synagogue.

In Bristol a courageous Jewish lady named Beatriz Nunes and her husband, a well-known physician, were the heart and soul of the secret Marrano community. They led the services, themselves baked the unleavened bread for Passover and brought over from distant lands Jewish books for the use of the Marranos.

At about this time the Marranos in Spain and Portugal were greatly harried by the Inquisition. This was a court of enquiry set up by the Catholic Church for discovering, among other things, whether the Jewish converts to Christianity were practising their Jewish faith in secret. The Inquisition had its torture chambers for forcing confessions from the unhappy victims. Those found guilty of practising Judaism were burnt at the stake.

Unhappily for the secret Jewish community in London at that time, a Marrano who was being tortured by the Inquisition in Portugal in 1542 revealed that there was a Marrano community in London. Very soon the Spanish court informed the English government of this. Those Marranos who had been in England for only a short period were arrested and their property seized. The others were not molested. Despite this, some departed of their own accord for fear of expulsion.

A notable visitor to England at this time was Mark Raphael a baptized Jew from Venice. He was invited by Henry VIII to come to England in order to advise him, the king, on the Jewish law of divorce. The Pope had refused to permit the king to be divorced from his wife Catherine of Aragon, on grounds based on the Hebrew Bible. The king thereupon sought advice from Raphael who was well versed in Jewish learning. There was an exciting attempt by the enemies of the king to kidnap Raphael and prevent him reaching London. However, all such efforts failed and Raphael arrived to add the weight of his knowledge to the king's advisers.

During the reign of Queen Elizabeth many Marranos were again settled in London, their leader being Hector Nunez, called popularly 'Doctor Hectour'. He was a physician as well as a great merchant and enjoyed the protection of the government. He it was who brought to Queen Elizabeth's minister, Lord Walsingham, the first news that the Spanish Armada had arrived at Lisbon on its way to the English Channel. 'Dr Hectour' was in close touch with Marranos in Spain and Portugal who at the risk of their own lives collected information about the plans of the Spaniards. These they passed on to the English government through their brethren in London. It was thus that Dr Hector Nunez and other Marranos in England were able to render important services to the country in those fateful days. At this time also, there was a small group of Italian Jews who, to win sympathy, passed in

England as Italian Protestants, refugees from Catholic persecution.

On one occasion a ship sailing from Portugal was captured by an English vessel. The passengers, who were Marranos fleeing from Spain and the Inquisition, were arrested and brought ashore. Among them was the beautiful Maria Nunez accompanied by her brother who were on their way to Amsterdam in order to return openly to the Jewish faith. Their parents had suffered at the hands of the Inquisition. Queen Elizabeth learning of the capture of the ship and its Marrano passengers, asked to see the beautiful Marrano. She was charmed with Maria and drove with her in the royal coach through the streets of London. The ship and its passengers were ordered to be set at liberty. Maria was invited by the queen to remain in England, but her heart was set on returning to the faith of her fathers. She declined the honour paid her by Queen Elizabeth and continued her journey to Amsterdam, where she returned openly to Judaism.

So far we have dealt mainly with Sephardi Jews – that is to say Jews from Spain and Portugal. But there were also Ashkenazi Jews, or Jews from Central and Eastern Europe, who found their way to England. One of these was Joachim Gaunse, a mining engineer from

Bohemia. He had come to England in 1581 with certain inventions concerning mining. For several years he carried on his work unmolested in the copper mines in Cumberland and Wales. Then one day in the year 1598, in an argument about religion, he cast doubt on Christianity and was arrested for blasphemy. Before the mayor of Bristol he defended himself by declaring he was a Jew born in Prague, had never been baptized and therefore not bound to accept the Christian belief. This saved him from punishment for blasphemy.

ELIZABETHAN LITERATURE

As we have seen, there was never a time in the Middle Period when there were no Jews in England. Nevertheless, they were so few in number that not many Englishmen had a knowledge of them. They knew more about Jews either through what they were told by Christian preachers, the popular ballads of little Saint Hugh (see p. 89), or what they read in books written by men who knew little of Jews, or what they saw acted in religious plays in which the Jew was always made the villian of the piece.

In stage plays the Jew was always shown with a huge red wig and a big false nose. The English writers gave their Jewish characters the parts of wicked men and evil-doers. No wonder, therefore, that when Jews began to come to England in larger numbers at the beginning of the sixteenth century, ordinary Englishmen looked on them with suspicion and dislike.

There are a number of English writings dating from the Middle Period which portray Jews. The most notable of these are Chaucer's Canterbury Tales, The Unfortunate Traveller by Thomas

Nashe, The Jew of Malta by Christopher Marlowe and The Merchant of Venice by William Shakespeare. In every one of these works the Jew is shown as a vile and unpleasant character. In the Canterbury Tales Chaucer brings in the story of Hugh of Lincoln and makes it appear that the Jews in the story told by the Prioress actually committed a murder as part of the practice of the Jewish religion. This shameful lie blackened the character of Jews among English people for more than two hundred years, for Chaucer's Tales were widely known and popular among the people. A long time passed before people came to know Jews and to understand that it was, indeed, a lie.

In Nashe's The Unfortunate Traveller, which was published in 1594, the two Jewish characters in the story are the blackest villains and scamps one can imagine. The scene is laid in Rome and the two Jews – one the Pope's physician and the other an apothecary – are made to spend their time in a constant bout of murder and poisoning.

It should be remembered that Thomas Nashe, the author, lived in the Elizabethan period, a period which was the finest in English literature, for it gave birth to such immortal writers as Shakespeare, Marlowe, Ben Johnson and many others. Nevertheless, despite the greatness of these writers, the picture of Jews drawn by them was false and degrading. The most striking of the Jewish characters drawn by the writers of the whole of the Middle Period is Shylock, in The Merchant of Venice, by William Shakespeare.

In fact, Shakespeare not only used an old Italian tale for the plot of The Merchant of Venice, but went out of his way to change the character of the Jew. In the Italian story which he used for his play, it is the Jew whose pound of flesh is demanded by the Christian merchant. But a play with such a plot would have caused an uproar in any English theatre at that period, and so Shakespeare made the Jew the villain of the piece and presented him as demanding the pound of flesh from the Christian. This was more to the liking of the English audience. Even so, the art and greatness of Shakespeare triumphed over the unfairness of the period. He put into the mouth of Shylock a number of great speeches which show that he felt deeply the tragedy of the Jew.

The most striking of these speeches is the following passage which shows that Shakespeare was not without sympathy for Jews and their sufferings when he makes Shylock exclaim: 'I am a Jew. Hath not a Jew eyes? Hath not a Jew hands, organs, dimensions, senses, affections, passions? Fed with the same food, hurt with the same weapons, subject to the same diseases, healed by the same winter and summer as a Christian is? If you prick us do we not bleed? If you tickle us do we not laugh? If you poison us do we not die? And if you wrong us, shall we not revenge?'

In The Jew of Malta, too, Christopher Marlowe presents a detestable character as a Jew. The scene of the play is laid in Malta, and Barabbas, the Jew, is drawn as a trickster, a rogue of the deepest dye. In the play as produced in the days of Elizabeth, the arrival of Barabbas on the stage in bright red wig and red false nose, was the signal for uproarious laughter. Marlowe's play was written and produced soon after the arrest in London of Roderigo Lopez, a Marrano, who was Queen Elizabeth's physician. Lopez is said to have been captured by Sir Francis Drake and brought to England where his skill as a doctor soon gained him fame and the coveted position of Court physician. He was also the first house physician of St Bartholomew's, in London, the oldest hospital in the kingdom.

His knowledge of Spain and family connections there made it possible for Lopez to supply the English government with plans of what the Spaniards were doing about the time when the Armada was in preparation. Nevertheless, neither his skill nor his services saved him from the envy and scheming of the Earl of Essex who planned his downfall. Lopez was arrested in 1593 on a charge of plotting against the Queen's life, and hanged at Tyburn on 7th June, 1594, without the charge ever having been proved. Papers found in recent years in Spain show, without any doubt, that Lopez was not a spy for the Spaniards, nor did he plot to murder the Queen. Indeed, modern historians declare that he was an innocent victim. Elizabeth herself wore till the day of her death a ring he had presented to her.

Lopez's execution and Marlowe's Jew of Malta did a great deal to give the people of England a wrong and most unfair impression of Jews.

THE BIBLE IN ENGLISH

The Authorized Version of the Bible is the pride and glory of the English tongue. It has shaped the language and character of the people more than any other single work. Jews played an important part in its making. The Old Testament could not be understood and faithfully translated except with the full knowledge of the Hebrew language. For this, the English translators, great scholars though they were, had to come to the learned Jews of the time and make use of the works of the Hebrew sages.

During the reign of Queen Mary many of the great Protestant scholars fled from England to the Continent to escape persecution. Some of them met there for the first time Jewish scholars from whom they learnt the Hebrew language and Jewish explanations of difficult parts of the Bible. When Elizabeth came to the throne and Protestantism was again supreme, the Protestant scholars returned to England carrying with them the knowledge they had gained abroad.

Indeed, the Hebrew language then flourished in England as never before or since. We know that many of the great lords and ladies of the time devoted themselves to the study of Hebrew. Among them were Queen Elizabeth and the ill-fated Lady Jane Grey.

Tremellius, a noted Hebrew scholar, came to England in 1547 and 1565. His work in England did a great deal to strengthen the foundations of Protestantism for he based it on scholarly interpretations of the Bible which differed in many respects from those of the Catholics. Tremellius himself was a convert, first to Catholicism and then to Protestantism. In later life he returned to the Jewish faith. He went back to his native Italy, declining to stay in England although pressed to so by Queen Elizabeth.

It was in the reign of James I that the Authorized Version of the Bible was completed. King James himself had a knowledge of Hebrew and helped in the translation.

The translation was followed by great changes in England. From that time onwards a knowledge of the Bible became common to all. Henceforth, ordinary tradesmen, townsmen and humble villagers could study and quote Holy Writ. It was this that very soon gave rise to the new sects such as the Puritans and the Quakers, which later had such a strong influence in the time of Cromwell.

In the struggle between Parliament and the

king, it was the ideas of justice and equality as taught in the Psalms and the Prophets of the Old Testament that gave strength to the side that eventually triumphed.

MANASSEH BEN ISRAEL

September, 1655, is a most important date in the history of the Jews of England. It marks the arrival in London of Rabbi Manasseh ben Israel, reputed as being the greatest rabbi of the day. He was described as a man of 'a middling stature and inclining to Fatness...His hair was very Grey...his Demeanor Graceful and Comely... He Commanded an aweful Reverence.' He came from Amsterdam in Holland to present his *Humble Address* a petition to Oliver Cromwell for the admission of Jews to England. In it he also asked for all the ancient laws against Jews to be abolished.

Until that time, although there were Jews in England, they were in the country under the guise of Spanish or Portuguese Catholics. They were the Marranos referred to in an earlier chapter. It was Manasseh ben Israel's object to get Cromwell to allow the Marranos not only to practise the Jewish religion openly, but also to permit Jews from abroad to come into the country openly as Jews.

Seven years before, in 1648, Eastern Europe

had been drenched with Jewish blood shed by the wild Cossacks of the Ukraine under their leader, or hetman, Bogdan Chmielnicki. Great Jewish communities throughout Poland had been ravaged and scattered. Thousands escaping massacre fled into Germany and Holland. Jewish leaders throughout Europe were faced with the terrible problem of finding new homes for these refugees.

At the same time, Marranos from Spain and Portugal continued to escape in considerable numbers from the tortures of the Inquisition, travelling mostly to Holland where they could live as Jews. Some of these made their way to England, but only the wealthy were able to travel far.

Rabbi Manasseh ben Israel felt the heavy burden of suffering and homelessness of his brethren. He had heard of the rise of the Puritans in England, and had met some of them in Holland. He had learnt with great satisfaction of their high regard for the Old Testament and the love these Englishmen bore for the people of the Bible. It was this that led him to come to England and attempt to secure from Oliver Cromwell permission for Jews to live in England openly as Jews.

Manasseh ben Israel's petition made a great stir in the land. Not all favoured the return of

I

the Jews, and many disliked the idea. In addition
the merchants of the City of London feared that
the Jewish merchants who might come into the
country, would, because of their connection
throughout the world, take their business from
them. There were others who were afraid of the
effects of Jewish teaching and the danger of many
Christians being turned to the Jewish faith
Pamphlets were written for and against Manasseh
ben Israel's petition and the subject was hotly
discussed. Many foresaw the fulfilment of
prophecy when the Jewish people would be re
established in the Holy Land. One writer, after
seeing Manasseh ben Israel, wrote: 'My heart
questions not the calling home of the nation of
the Jews. Thou wilt hasten it, Oh my God . .
of the ends of the whole world, hasten it, Amen!
Another writer puts down the sufferings of the
Civil War to divine punishment for the bad treat
ment of the English Jews before the Expulsion.

On 12th November, 1655, Manasseh presented
his *Humble Address* in person to Oliver Cromwell
at the Council of State in Whitehall. A com
mittee was appointed by the Council to consider
it. The London populace was excited by all kind
of startling rumours. The most fantastic of these
was that the Jews had offered half-a-million
pounds to buy St Paul's Cathedral for turning
into a synagogue.

On December 4th, 1655, a Conference presided over by Cromwell himself, met in Whitehall to discuss whether it was lawful to admit the Jews. The cleverest English judges and lawyers were present. They declared that there was no law which forbade the return of the Jews to England. They stated further that the Expulsion in 1290 had been at the order of the king and was not an act of Parliament, and so not a law of the land for all time.

This fact surprised many people. But the Conference having made sure of this, had to decide on what terms to allow the Jews into England. This was not so easy to settle, for the hostile pamphlets had done their work and base rumours had worked their mischief. Hatred of Jews was fanned by bigoted and fanatical people. Again the fear was expressed of the Jewish religion drawing people away from Christianity; the clergy were opposed and tradesmen feared for their livelihood, not understanding that Jews would bring in new trades, so that commerce would increase for everyone. It was a bitter disappointment to Cromwell whose favourable opinion of the Jews was based on their great abilities. He understood the advantages they could bring with them and was ashamed that English merchants should allow their selfishness to stand in the way both of the country's progress and the welfare of the Jews.

When one member of the Conference suggested that Jews be admitted to neglected ports and towns to make these prosperous, and that they should pay twice as heavy taxes as Christian merchants, Cromwell rose in wrath from his seat. Turning to the merchants present at the Conference, he addressed them in scornful and angry tones, crying: 'You say that the Jews are the meanest and most despised of all people ... But in that case, what becomes of your fears? Can you really be afraid that this people should be able to prevail in trade and credit over the merchants of England?'

Despite Cromwell's goodwill he could not overcome the hostility of the Conference, which he dismissed. Although he never granted formal recognition for the re-admission of the Jews, it was connived at obliquely, and was in fact achieved as a result of the Robles case.

Antonio Rodrigues Robles had his property confiscated as a Spanish national which status he disclaimed. The matter was eventually decided on the grounds of religion. Robles's property was returned to him – as a Spanish Catholic he did not have rights in England, but as a refugee Jew his position was secure.

Menasseh ben Israel however returned to Holland to die a disappointed man, for he had hoped for a proper edict of re-admission and not this rather vague legal toleration. Before leaving England he published a noble vindication, or defence of the Jews, in Latin.

About this time war broke out between England and Spain and the confiscation was ordered of some of the property of the Marranos who were still regarded as Spanish citizens. The brilliant Defence of the Jews by Manasseh ben Israel had, however, strengthened the courage of the Marranos. They themselves presented a petition to Cromwell which was signed by Manasseh and others, declaring that they were not Spaniards but members of the Jewish nation. In this they were successful and their petition was accepted. For the first time they were officially recognized as Jews.

Following this they openly rented a house in Creechurch Lane, in the City of London, as a synagogue: for the first time in three centuries there was an official Jewish house of prayer in England.

Shortly after a plot of land was rented in Mile End, then on the outskirts of London, as a cemetery. Until that time the secret Jews of England had either buried their dead in consecrated grounds in private gardens, or transported their bodies to Holland.

Although Manasseh ben Israel failed to obtain

official permission for Jews from abroad to settle in England, his work resulted in an improvement in the position of the Marranos. They were now allowed to practise the Jewish religion openly and were no longer bound to go about in the guise of Spanish or Portuguese Catholics or Protestant refugees. But Manasseh was far from satisfied. He continued to implore Cromwell to grant his petition, and did not tire in his efforts to persuade men of influence in England to help him.

Manasseh ben Israel returned to Holland in 1657, a sorely disappointed man. He died, at the age of 53, two months after his return little knowing that his efforts had laid the foundation for a great and prosperous Jewish community in these isles.

PART III
THE MODERN PERIOD
from Charles II to 1967

CHARLES II 1660-1685
and
JAMES II 1685-1688

Oliver Cromwell, Lord Protector of England, died in September, 1658. During the short period of the rule of his son Richard before the restoration of the monarchy and Charles II's restoration the land was in a state of confusion.

The Jews of England feared that the passing of Cromwell would bring with it the loss of the protection which they had obtained. Indeed, an anti-Jewish party had already begun to arouse hatred against them and demanded their expulsion from the land.

On the restoration of the monarchy two places of worship were already established: the Sephardi synagogue in Creechurch Lane and an Ashkenazi house of prayer in St Helens, both in the City of London. The Sephardi one was strongly built, and for protection against surprise had three doors, one inside the other, each with two locks. The synagogue consisted of two rooms, the smaller one for women, the rooms being separated by a partition in which was fixed a long narrow window. Through this window the women could observe and follow the services.

An English Christian, John Greenhalgh by name, visited this synagogue in April, 1662. He describes the lively scene at the service at which there were present more than a hundred Jews, 'most of them rich in apparel, divers with jewels glittering'. The women, too, were in handsome array, wearing silks trimmed with broad gold lace, a muff in one hand, a prayer-book in the other. 'I confess,' writes Greenhalgh, 'that looking earnestly upon them in this, and thoughts coming into my mind of the wonders which God wrought for their fathers in Egypt . . . I was strangely, uncouthly, unaccustomedly moved, and deeply affected: tears stood in my eyes to see those banished Sons of Israel . . . in a strange land . . .' He was also much impressed by the knowledge of Hebrew shown by the young boys present; and adds that 'the right true Hebrew Tongue' was taught from earliest infancy to the Jewish children of the Restoration period. A special schoolmistress was employed for this sole purpose.

No sooner was Charles on the throne than the Christian city merchants petitioned him to expel the Jews. They were headed by the Lord Mayor and City Corporation. The small Jewish community, knowing how quickly the mob might be roused against them, shut themselves up in their houses and refused to see any strangers. As a forlorn hope, however, they decided to send an address, to the king. In it they did not disguise the fact that they were living in England as Jews, and prayed for permission to reside in the king's dominions.

The petition against them, as well as their own address was read at the Privy Council and the king later sent the address to the House of Commons in a manner which showed that his sympathy was with the Jews. Parliament too, took no action and no answer was sent to the petition by the City merchants. The result was that the Jewish position remained as it was before the death of Cromwell.

King Charles, whose queen, Catherine of Braganza, brought with her to England a Jewish physician, Dr Fernando Mendez, had thus proved his tolerance. He had also fulfilled a promise made by him to the Jews of Amsterdam while in exile from his kingdom. At the same time as Manasseh ben Israel was in England seeking permission for Jews to live in London, the Jews of Amsterdam had given considerable help to Charles. In gratitude he promised that when he was restored to the throne he would give them his protection.

The enemies of the Jews did not give up hope of harming them. There was a law in force forbidding assemblies for prayer, except for members of the Church of England. The law was really passed against Nonconformists and Catholics, that is Christians who were not members of the Church of England. Nevertheless, the enemies of the Jews attempted to make use of this law to have the services in the synagogues stopped. The more wicked ones, among them the Earl of Berkshire, tried to extort money by blackmail from the small Jewish community, threatening to use the law against them unless they paid out a large sum.

The community again sent a petition to the king asking for the protection of the law. This was examined by the Privy Council and an answer was returned on August 22nd, 1664, declaring that no orders had been given to disturb them and that they could expect '... the same favour as formerly they have had,' so long as they lived peaceably 'with due obedience to his Majesty's law, and without scandal to his Government.'

This stated for the first time in writing that the Jewish residence in England was rightful and could not be disturbed. The uncertainty and the anxiety which had hung over them so long were, except for one more incident in the next reign, finally removed. It marks the end of what we have described as the Middle Period in the history of the Jews of England. From that time onward there was a steady increase in the rights of Jews in the kingdom. Nevertheless their British citizenship in the full sense of the word was not to come about till many years had passed.

Charles II was followed by James II, the last of the Stuart kings. His short reign of three years continued the peace and favour which the Jews of England had enjoyed under Charles, his brother. Like him, James took a strong stand when an attempt was made to interfere with the free religious observance of the Jews. In 1685 some evil-minded persons thought of a method of harming Jews through a law passed in the reign of Queen Elizabeth which imposed a fine for absence from church. Although it was aimed against Catholics who failed to attend Church of England services, the enemies of the Jews planned to set the law moving against them. One day thirty-seven Jews were arrested at the Royal Exchange while on business, on the charge of failing to attend church service. Once again the community petitioned the king. James, as resolute as his brother, issued an order stopping any action against the Jews and commanding that they were not to be disturbed in the practise of their religion. Never again were the Jews of England molested on this account.

THE COLONIES

While some Jews were slowly improving their position in England, others from Europe had gone out as pioneers to take part in the founding of new colonies in the West Indies and on the mainland of the American continent.

The first Europeans to settle in the American continent came from Spain and Portugal. The expedition under Columbus that discovered America (see page 113) was a Spanish expedition and Columbus took possession of the territory in the name of the King of Spain. Very soon men and women were streaming across the Atlantic from Spain to found new homes. Among them were both openly practising Jews and Marranos. It is not surprising therefore to find that Jews played an important part in the growth of the new colonies.

Spain and Portugal were not, however, left long as the only powers in the New World. Intrepid explorers sailed from England and Holland to discover new islands and territories on the American mainland and to challenge Spain's power. The wars between the different countries in Europe spread to the New World and soon we find the lands on the American continent split up under the ownership of Spain, Portugal, Holland, England and France.

The buccaneers from England harried the Spanish Main. In their raids they frequently sacked the Spanish settlements and seized their galleons. Scattered throughout the Spanish islands and parts of the New World, the Marranos watched eagerly the growing challenge to the power of Spain. More than once, when the buccaneers struck at Spain, Marranos in the islands and on the mainland came forward to help them and thus avenge themselves on their hated persecutors.

The cruel Inquisition was carried by the Spaniards and Portuguese from Europe to America. Marranos who had gone to the New World hoping to be able to practise openly the Jewish faith in safety, soon found that they had either to continue under the guise of Catholics or to face death at the stake. Many chose martyrdom and were burnt at the stake, proclaiming the Unity of the God of Israel as the fire consumed them. Others remained hidden as Marranos until parts of the New World came into the possession of the Protestant governments of England and Holland. Thither they made their way with their families and goods.

The first colony in the New World in which Jews lived openly as Jews was the Island of Barbados – one of the group of islands known as the West Indies. Among the other important islands of the group are Cuba and Jamaica. The former remained in the possession of Spain until the nineteenth century, and the Marranos in that island suffered cruelly at the hands of the Inquisition. Jamaica passed into British possession in 1655.

Barbados was discovered by the English in 1605, and settled by them some twenty years later. Jews were among the earliest colonists and by 1628 were already playing an important part in the island.

While in England at this time Jews had still to conceal their Jewishness, they were allowed to practise their religion freely in Barbados. From time to time, little groups of Jews arrived here from disturbed parts of the New World, as well as from Europe. Within a short time the Jews of Barbados had increased the wealth of the island and made it into a prosperous possession of the motherland.

Jamaica was taken from the Portuguese by Cromwell in 1655. When Columbus discovered the New World this island was given to him as a reward by the Spanish sovereign. He did not allow – perhaps because he was himself a

Marrano or of Marrano descent – the Inquisition to carry on its cruel work in Jamaica. This freedom from persecution attracted many Marranos to the island and although they were known to be Jews under the mask of Catholics they were not molested. Nevertheless, they longed for the day when they could worship the God of Israel openly and without fear.

The day of freedom came for the Marranos when an English expedition captured the island in 1655. The conquest was assisted by the Marranos of Jamaica. The English fleet was piloted into the harbour of Kingston, now the capital, by a Jewish sea captain, Campoe Sabatho by name.

The conquest and the settlement of Jamaica after its capture was also helped by Simon de Caceres, a Marrano from London. He was highly valued by Cromwell for the valuable information he obtained for him from Spain and the Spanish and Portuguese possessions in the New World. This same Simon de Caceres had great plans for freeing the Marranos and enabling them to fight as Jews against the Spanish oppressors in the New World. He proposed to Cromwell the formation of a Jewish army for the conquest of Chile in South America.

The English conquest of Jamaica attracted other Jews to the island. After Cromwell's death,

K

Charles II continued to treat the Jews of Jamaica fairly and they prospered. On one occasion, in 1671, some Christian merchants, envious of the Jews, petitioned the English government to expel them from Jamaica. But Governor Lynch of the island advised the king not to grant the petition because of the value of the Jews to the growing colony. The result was that the petition was not only rejected, but the king ordered that still more Jews should be encouraged to settle in Jamaica.

It was about this time that Surinam, one of the English colonies in the West Indies, was captured by the Dutch. Surinam was originally a Portuguese colony and the Dutch had taken it from them. When the English occupied it in 1655 they found there a prosperous Jewish community which had enjoyed full rights under the Dutch Government. The English continued these rights until the island passed again into Dutch hands. When this occurred the English insisted on the Dutch allowing the Jews to depart with them, so that they could be settled in other British possessions, for they did not wish to lose their valuable services. On the other hand, the Dutch insisted on the Jews remaining with them for the same reason; and although Charles II sent three ships to carry the Jews of Surinam to Jamaica, the Dutch governor would not allow them to depart.

In 1664, an English fleet captured the colony of New Amsterdam from the Dutch and renamed it New York. This in the course of time became one of the world's largest cities, containing more Jews than any other city in the world. Before its capture by the English, the Jews of New Amsterdam had succeeded in gaining full rights. Under the treaty following the capture, the Dutch insisted that all citizens of New Amsterdam should be granted freedom of worship and this applied also to the Jews. At that time Jews were already settled, not only in New York, but in Rhode Island, Maryland and scattered places throughout North America.

WILLIAM III 1689–1702

William of Orange (William III) ascended the throne of England in 1689. He came at the invitation of Protestant England after James II had fled the country.

In Holland William had been the Stadtholder, or head of the State. This country which had a powerful and wealthy Jewish community was the centre of the Marranos who when they wished to return openly to the faith of their fathers made their way to Amsterdam from Spain and Portugal.

It is said that William found his expedition to England for accepting the throne held up at the last moment because of lack of means. A group of Amsterdam Jews raised a large loan for the government of Holland on behalf of William.

With William there came to England a number of prominent Jews who had helped greatly in the prosperity of Holland.

William was now both king of England and ruler of Holland. The two countries were thus under the same ruler, and this made easier the passage backwards and forwards of the leading Jews of both countries.

The Jews of Holland had helped greatly in building up the Dutch empire. Among them were sea captains, leaders of the Dutch East India Company, great doctors and writers of renown. They soon began to take an active part in the life of the Jewish community in England.

The first Jew, openly practising Judaism, ever to receive an English knighthood, was Solomon de Medina. He came from Holland with William III and was soon a great army contractor and organized supplies for the armies of the Duke of Marlborough in the War of the Spanish Succession.

Till now the Jewish arrivals in England had been mainly wealthy Sephardim. They came, often with great sums of money, and as partners in wealthy companies with agencies throughout Europe, the New World and even the Far East. There were, however, numbers of poor Jews, refugees from persecution in different parts of Europe who, hearing of the prosperity of English Jews, made their way to these shores. Nearly all of these were Ashkenazi Jews (see page 130). They were not so cultured in the worldly sense as the Sephardim, although they carried with them vast stores of Talmudic learning and knowledge of the Torah. Unlike their Sephardi brethren the Ashkenazim had never at any time passed as anything but Jews. It was this that made it more difficult for them to enter new countries and to take root in places where there were as yet no Jewish communities to receive them.

You will remember that when Rabbi Manasseh ben Israel came to England, he was seeking to obtain refuge for Jews who were practising their religion openly, both Sephardi and Ashkenazi Jews. The latter were at that time suffering from the cruel massacres under the Cossack bandit Bogdan Chmielnicki in the Ukraine, and Manasseh had seen large numbers of homeless Jews arriving in the Dutch towns. Since then the Ashkenazi Jews had spread into other parts of Europe. Some of them arrived, weary and penniless on English soil during the reigns of Charles II and James II. Without the chance of working in English trades, they took to peddling for a living trudging with their packs from village to village and covering the whole country, in an endeavour to sell their small wares.

In 1677 the steady increase in the number of poor Jews alarmed the Corporation of the City of London. The Aldermen of the City considered the matter and decided that no Jew without sufficient means was to be allowed to live in London. They were, however, free to settle in other cities. The result was that numbers of Jews went to other places, particularly the ports, such as Bristol, Hull and Portsmouth.

Nevertheless the Ashkenazi Jews in London increased in numbers. They had as yet no separate regular synagogue of their own, only a house of prayer, although their pronunciation of Hebrew was different from that of the Sephardim and there were also certain small differences in the synagogue services. The Sephardim treated them as inferiors, allowing them none of the honours given in their synagogues, and no voice in the management of the affairs of the community. They did, however, help the Ashkenazi poor from their own charity funds.

In 1690 a number of wealthier Ashkenazi merchants who had come mostly from Hamburg, established a separate synagogue in Mitre Square, in the City of London. The Sephardi and Ashkenazi congregations remained on friendly terms and as you will see later, acted together in times of trouble. The Sephardi community had, in the meantime, outgrown their small synagogue in Creechurch Lane in the City of London. They decided to build a great and beautiful house of prayer and began the building of the new synagogue in 1699 on a plot of land in Bevis Marks, on the boundary of the City. It is related that the builder, a Quaker, Joseph Avis by name, returned all the profit he had made on the building when the synagogue was opened, declaring that he would not keep for himself any profit made out of erecting a house of prayer. The new synagogue, popularly known as Bevis Marks, was consecrated in 1702. Into the ceiling of this synagogue was built one of the timbers of a man-of-war, presented by Queen Anne. The beautiful brass hanging lamps were brought from Holland, while many of the benches and other fittings came from the old synagogue in Creechurch Lane.

The Sephardim were very proud of their fine synagogue which was called by the Hebrew name of *Sh-ar haShamayim,* or, in English, Gate of Heaven, from the words of Jacob after he was awakened from the dream, at Bethel, of angels descending to earth. The name was taken from the verse, 'This is none other than the house of God and this is the Gate of Heaven'.

For many years, on the eve of the Day of Atonement, prayers were offered up in this synagogue on behalf 'of our brethren who are imprisoned in the dungeons of the Inquisition'.

The Sephardim could boast a number of *Hahams,* or learned men and scholars. The word *Haham* is a Hebrew word meaning a sage. It is the title Sephardim given to learned men and rabbis. The first of the English *Hahams* was Rabbi Jacob Sasportas who came to London in 1664, having at one time served as ambassador from the ruler of Morocco to the king of Spain.

He was followed by other learned rabbis. The most noted of them, David Nieto, became *Haham* of the Sephardim in 1701. He was a profound scholar of the Torah, as well as a noted physician and astronomer. He ably defended the strict letter of the Jewish religion.

The Ashkenazim, too, had learned rabbis and scholars. The earliest was Rabbi Yehudah ben Ephraim Cohen. There was not, however, any chief rabbi of the Ashkenazim till many years later.

QUEEN ANNE 1702–1714

When William III died in 1702 the Sephardi and
Ashkenazi communities were two distinct bodies.
Each had its own synagogue; the Sephardim a
stately house of prayer, the Ashkenazim a humble
place of worship in Mitre Square, both in the City
of London.

During the reign of Queen Anne, who succeeded William, the Jews of England continued
to grow in numbers and importance. Arrivals
from the Continent increased year by year,
especially Ashkenazi Jews from Germany and
Poland. The small house of prayer in Mitre
Square was added to by numbers of small prayer-
houses which were used for the study of Talmud
by the grown-ups, as well as classrooms for the
children.

But officially there was still one Ashkenazi congregation till 1706. In that year a separate congregation was set up by a number of Hamburg
merchants who worshipped at a house in Magpie
Alley not far from Mitre Square. Among them
was Mordecai Hamburger, also known as Marcus
Moses, the son-in-law of Glückel of Hamelin

whose interesting autobiography is now a Jewish classic.

By now the Ashkenazi community had among its members a number of wealthy and learned men who could vie with some of the pillars of the Sephardi congregation. The trade in precious stones was largely in their hands. Some of them had connections as far afield as India and Brazil in South America. Nevertheless, the Sephardim still held aloof from them and many years were to pass before they were to regard their brethren from Eastern Europe as equals in every respect.

During the reign of Queen Anne there were still some signs that those who were opposed to Jewish freedom in Britain had not given up their efforts against the Jews. An Act was passed by Parliament in 1702, forcing Jewish parents to supply the needs of any of their children, even when grown up, who had been converted to the Christian faith.

GEORGE I 1714–1727

The accession of George I in 1714 marks the beginning of the Hanoverian royal family. From that family are descended all the sovereigns of Great Britain until this day. George I's ascent to the throne did not come about without a serious disturbance in the country. There occurred what is known as the Jacobite rising; the Jacobites were supporters of the Old Pretender, the son of James II, who claimed the throne of England. Jews were not affected by this rebellion, remaining loyal to the king chosen by Parliament and the country.

There was, however, a case of a single Jew, Francis Francia by name, known as the 'Jew Jacobite', who was tried in London, in 1716, on a charge of aiding the supporters of the Old Pretender. He was born in France. At the trial he revealed himself as an observant Jew for he refused to take the oath excepting with covered head and on a Hebrew sacred book. He was found not guilty of plotting against the king and was set free.

Four years later, in 1720, England was thrown

into consternation by what is known as the South Sea Bubble. This is the name given to a period of reckless gambling on the Stock Exchange and of raising money for companies for all kinds of fantastic ventures. Every section of the population was affected by the temptation of gaining riches quickly. It is related that Jews alone remained cool-headed and were not drawn into the general fever of spending and gambling. Indeed, although a very large number of people were ruined during the period of the South Sea Bubble, there is not a single Jewish name among them.

The reign of George I brought with it a considerable spread of commerce and the invention of new ideas in business and industry. Among the most important, because it helped to give England a start in the rise of the mercantile marine, was the scheme for the insuring against the loss of ships and cargo. This plan was the idea of a Jew, Philip Heilbuth, and led to the founding of Lloyds, famous throughout the world to this day for the insurance of ships and cargoes.

It is interesting to note that insurance of ships was no new idea among Jews. It is actually mentioned in the Talmud and goes back at least 1700 years.

King George I had come from Hanover in Germany to England. His arrival had also attracted German and other Jews from the Con-

tinent. These were Ashkenazi Jews. The increase
in the number of Ashkenazim which had begun
in the previous reign was now even more marked.
Numbers of them had become wealthy and resolved to set up a synagogue which would not be
less in dignity than that of their Sephardi
brethren and provide space for their growing
number of worshippers.

In 1722 the Ashkenazim erected a spacious
synagogue in Duke's Place, Aldgate within the
bounds of the City of London, not far distant
from the Sephardi synagogue in Bevis Marks. In
the same year Uri Phaibush, also known as Aaron
Hart, became rabbi of the Ashkenazi congregation which now had its centre in Duke's Place
synagogue, the name by which it was popularly
called.

Another Ashkenazi synagogue, an enlarged and
finer outgrowth of the one in Magpie Alley was
completed in 1726. It was known as the Hambro'
(i.e. Hamburg) Synagogue.

The Ashkenazi Jews, now risen to importance,
no longer submitted so readily to the superior
claims of the Sephardim. They made every effort
to assert their independence and dignity. They
established their own charities, including a
Talmud Torah school which was set up in 1732.
This separation from the Sephardim could not be
avoided, for the Ashkenazim and the Sephardim

spoke different languages among themselves. They had different customs, for their history had differed greatly through many centuries. While the Sephardim spoke classic Portuguese and the Spanish of Castile, the Ashkenazim spoke Yiddish, a language based on old German with many Hebrew and Slavonic words, and written and printed in the Hebrew characters.

GEORGE II 1727–1760

On the accession of George II to the throne, the community was faced with the problem of the large number of poor Jews in the country. These had come from Europe where life was difficult for Jews. They had heard of the prosperity of their brethren in England, of the many rich merchants and of the kindly treatment enjoyed by English Jews in comparison with the persecutions abroad. It was this that attracted Jewish immigrants from other lands. Most of them came without money and without knowledge of any trade or profession. Those from Eastern Europe, Ashkenazim, did not find in England as many Ashkenazim of great wealth as was the case with the Sephardim. The Ashkenazi charities did not have large funds at their disposal; nevertheless the Sephardi community contributed greatly to the support of the Ashkenazi poor. But both congregations were alarmed at the increase in the numbers of poor Jews in London for they feared the effect of this on the non-Jewish population if they were to need gentile charity and become charges on the poor law. They therefore tried to

The Boxer, Daniel Mendoza

Jewish Pedlar, 1823

deal with the problem in two ways. It was their aim to disperse the immigrants throughout the country, or encourage them to go abroad. Those who had no trades and were resolved to stay in England, were supplied with means for setting up as small traders and pedlars. It became a common sight at this period to see Jewish pedlars tramping the countryside with their packs of merchandise strapped on their backs. These pedlars formed the earliest Jewish congregations in the smaller English cities – such as Canterbury, Chatham, Southampton and Exeter.

Plans for getting poor Jews to go abroad did not prove successful. The main reason was that there were no countries willing to receive them and no large funds for their settlement. There did, however, arise from time to time friendly Englishmen who attempted to influence the government and the people in support of plans for helping Jews to emigrate. In 1732 Colonel Oglethorpe started the settlement of the colony of Georgia, in America. He obtained a charter for the purpose from the Crown, but the scheme was intended for the settlement of poor Englishmen and dissenters – that is to say persons who though not belonging to the Church of England, were not members of the Catholic faith. Jews could be counted as dissenters, although no special mention of them was made in the Charter. The

L

funds for the settlement in Georgia were supplied both by a grant from Parliament and by charitable gifts. Among those entrusted with the task of raising funds were the leading members of the Sephardi community – Alvaro Lopez Suasso, Francis Salvador and Anthony da Costa. These received gifts from other Jews. But instead of handing over these funds for general use, they devoted the money to sending out to Georgia a shipload of poor immigrant Jews who had arrived in England. This was opposed by those in charge of the scheme of settlement, and the three Jews were relieved of their posts.

The first batch of Jewish settlers, numbering forty in all, arrived in Georgia almost at the same time as the earliest English colonists. A year later a community of Sephardi Jews again tried to encourage Jewish emigration. They applied to the government for a grant of land in Carolina solely for the settlement of Jews. This was refused.

Some years later, in 1748, a scheme for settling 300,000 Jewish families in the Cherokee mountains in America, was presented to Parliament by Sir Alexander Cuming. This, too, came to nothing.

By this time there had grown up a generation of Jews born in England and mixing easily with their gentile neighbours. Many were already distinguished in the life of the country and were prominent as merchants and financiers, helping to develop the foreign trade introduced by the first settlers during Cromwell's rule. But prejudice against the Jew was still rife. In 1732, the English Jews were reminded by a sudden outburst of feeling against them that their position in the country was far from secure. A certain Osborne published a pamphlet containing a malicious invention that Portuguese Jews had murdered a Portuguese Jewess and her child because the father of the child was a Christian. This made-up story was sufficient to inflame the London rabble. Jews were attacked in the streets and went in fear of their lives, until Osborne was arrested, brought before the Court of Justice and the whole story was publicly disproved.

Jews born in England were without the full rights of citizens. They could not hold land and were not officially citizens of the country. It was only by conversion to Christianity that these rights could be obtained and it is this that explains why some wealthy Jews at this time left the Jewish faith. Only in the British American colonies had Jews been granted the full rights of citizenship. But it was not before 1740 that these rights were given the force of law by an Act of Parliament. The same law granted these rights also to Jews who had served at least two years in the navy or on British merchant ships during the war of the Spanish Succession. It seemed that Parliament was gradually turning in favour of the Jews of England. Among the better educated classes, especially among the clergy, there were Englishmen who sympathized with Jews in their sufferings in foreign countries and frequently preached and wrote in their defence. This sympathy took practical form in 1744 when the Jews of Prague, in Bohemia, appealed to their brethren in England for help in preventing their expulsion from that city, which had been decreed by the Empress Maria Theresa of Austria.

The appeal from Prague came to the Ashkenazi community in London. Straightaway the Ashkenazi leaders, Moses Hart and Aaron Franks, petitioned to see the king. George II received them without delay. The king was deeply moved by the news of the expulsion and listened with tears in his eyes to the story that the Jews had been driven from Prague because of an offence said to have been committed against Maria Theresa's rule by the Jews of Alsace, in France, many hundreds of miles away. It is related that the king showed profound emotion, declaring warmly, while the tears stood in his eyes, 'It is not right that the innocent should suffer for the guilty'. This led to the English ambassador in Vienna intervening with the Austrian government.

But as though to show that their feet were not

yet firmly set on English soil, the Jews of England received a shock in the same year when a bequest for founding a Jewish Talmudical college in London, was declared illegal by the courts. The judges described the purpose, the establishing of a *yeshiva*, of the bequest as a superstitious institute. As a result the Talmudical college was not founded and the money that had been left for the purpose was passed on by the courts for the use of the Foundlings' Hospital in London.

In 1745 the country was shaken by the rising under the Young Pretender, known as Bonnie Prince Charlie. The prince landed in the West Highlands of Scotland and put himself at the head of an army which marched south in order to depose George II. In London there was a panic which grew as the army of Prince Charlie drew nearer. The value of government loans or stock fell so low that people who owned them rushed to sell out. This added to the panic and further endangered the government. It meant that people were losing faith in the government and in its promise to repay loans raised from the people.

Bank of England notes fell in value, so that people would not accept them for money, except at much lower than their value. It was then that the Jewish community played an important part in helping to stem the panic and assist the State. The most notable Jewish financier of that time was Samson Gideon. Neither he nor the other Jewish financiers with him would accept Banknotes except at their true value. They helped the government by publicly importing gold into England. This showed the people that there was enough gold to pay out for every Banknote which anyone wished to exchange for cash. Samson Gideon also raised a loan of £1,700,000 for the needs of the government at that difficult time. The poorer Jews, too, played their part. Together with their wealthier brethren they joined the militia raised for defending the capital.

By the end of 1746, Bonnie Prince Charlie had been driven out of England and had become a fugitive. The country was again safe. Samson Gideon and his friends gained a great reputation for the assistance they had rendered the country in its hour of need.

Samson Gideon's name was now famous. Born in England in 1699 of Sephardi parents, he was known in the synagogue by the name of Samson de Rehuel Abudiente. At an early age he became a stockbroker and quickly grew to great wealth. It is told of him that at the beginning of the panic in 1745, he spent all his money on buying up government stock that was then falling in value. He was resolved to raise public trust by showing that be believed that Bonnie Prince Charlie would be defeated and that government stock would not lose its value. When his money was almost exhausted, a certain non-Jewish banker, Mr Snow, demanded that Gideon should immediately return to him a loan of £20,000. This sum had been lent to Gideon before the rising. At this time Bonnie Prince Charlie was approaching Derby, on his way to London and Mr Snow feared for his money. Indeed, the king himself feared for the future and was preparing to flee from London. When Gideon received Mr Snow's demand, he went to the Bank of England, obtained twenty banknotes each of the value of £1,000, wrapped them round a bottle of smelling salts and sent them to the quaking Mr Snow.

Unhappily, Samson Gideon later left the Jewish community without joining the Church. He wished to secure a lordly title for his family, and Jews could not at that time bear titles of nobility, but Gideon had married out so his children were Christians. His eldest son, while yet a lad, was given the title of baronet which could not be given to Gideon himself because he was still a Jew. Gideon served the government for many years with his advice on matters of finance and taxation. The Chancellor of the Exchequer and other ministers eagerly sought his counsel. When he died in 1763, it was discovered that Samson Gideon had continued as a member of the

Sephardi synagogue all the years since his separation from it. He was buried in the ancient Jewish cemetery at Mile End, London. His memory is recalled on every Yom Kippur, the Day of Atonement, among the lists of names recited in the prayer for the dead at the Bevis Marks synagogue.

That so powerful and wealthy a man as Samson Gideon should have had need for hiding his loyalty to the Jewish faith on account of a title and for securing the future of his family, shows that however happily placed, the Jews of England were still far from enjoying full rights. Not only Jews in England were without full rights, but also English-born Catholics and foreign Protestants. The Catholics had been gradually deprived of their rights ever since the Reformation. Foreign-born Protestants, however, made an effort to secure naturalization which would enable them to become English citizens if they wished. For the Jews of England these efforts were of importance. If successful they would encourage Jews to make a like effort. A naturalization bill for foreign Protestants was brought into Parliament in 1745 but was not passed. On that occasion a number of Sephardi Jews sought advice from the government as to whether the bill for foreign Protestants might not be changed so as to include Jews. They were, however, advised that the time for this was not yet ripe. They therefore decided to proceed gradually and hit on the idea of getting a naturalization act in Ireland which at that time had a separate Parliament, though under the Crown of England. For this purpose, the London Sephardim set up a special council of five members, known as the Committee of Diligence. So wisely did they do their work and so friendly was the Irish Parliament that the bill was passed in Dublin. It did not, however, become law as it did not receive the Royal signature of assent.

Nevertheless, there was no slackening in the effort to secure naturalization for Jews in England. Moreover times were changing, and there were many Christian Englishmen who were resolved to gain for the Jews of England the same rights as were enjoyed by Englishmen of the Christian faith.

In April 1753, a bill was passed in both Houses of Parliament which made it possible for foreign-born Jews to become British citizens. But so deep was the London mob's suspicion of foreigners of all kinds, that riots against the Jews broke out as soon as the bill was passed. Walls were plastered with slogans against the Jews. One of the most popular of these was: 'No Jews; no wooden shoes.'

In those days there were numbers of French Protestants who had taken refuge in England. These frequently wore distinctive wooden shoes resembling clogs known as sabots. The rhyme,

'No Jews; no wooden shoes,' was aimed both at Jews and foreign Christians.

It must be said to the credit of certain Christian Englishmen that they took the part of the Jews. Some clergymen preached sermons in their defence and were attacked in the street when recognized by the mob. There were also Englishmen who published pamphlets in their favour.

Fearing that these disturbances would inflict more injury on the Jews than could be made good by the Naturalization Act, parliament repealed the Act six months after it had become law.

Towards the end of George II's reign, the Jewish community in England had become the most powerful of all the Jewish communities throughout the world. Their numbers had increased, many of them had become wealthy. Some were prominent in the arts and sciences. They had also spread to the British possessions on the American continent. They were present at the conquest of Canada in 1760. In the older American colonies, Jews were to be found in all walks of life and taking part in the early pioneering and the Indian wars.

The Bevis Marks synagogue as the centre of the wealthy Sephardi congregation, was the symbol of the English community. The Elders of this congregation ruled their community with a firm hand, for they were being continually increased by arrivals of Marranos from the Continent, and special care had to be taken to make sure that the faith of Israel was kept undefiled by alien practices. It must be remembered that the dread Spanish Inquisition was still in force and the Elders of Bevis Marks had to take special care in admitting new arrivals to membership of the congregation for fear they might be spies of the Inquisition come to inform against Marranos in Spain and Portugal by uncovering their connection with their Jewish relatives in London. Indeed, in those days, prayers were recited regularly in Bevis Marks synagogue for the Jews who lay in the dungeons of the Inquisition suffering torture for their faith.

Among the noble services which Bevis Marks synagogue rendered to Jews of that time was the ransom of Jews captured by pirates in the Mediterranean. In those days the Barbary coast of North Africa was infested by pirates' lairs. The Barbary pirates would lie in wait for ships in these waters, seize the passengers and crew and sell them into slavery in Africa, unless they were ransomed. In order to save from slavery Jews who might be seized by the pirates, Bevis Marks synagogue appointed a special official called the Warden of the Captives, whose duty it was to arrange for the ransom of captive Jews.

GEORGE III 1760–1820

The first Jewish event on George III's accession to the throne marks the beginning of one of the most important Jewish institutions. Out of that event rose what is known as the Board of Deputies, the parliament of the Jews of the British Isles, as well as some of the British possessions beyond the seas.

It was the custom when a new king came to the throne for the Jews to send several of their most respected men with an address of loyalty to the Crown. You will remember that even long before this time, in 1189, the Jews of England sent their representatives with a loyal address and gifts to Richard I, on his coronation day, an unhappy day which led to massacres and sufferings of the Jews of those times (see page 54). Times were now very different and happier.

On George III's succession, the Sephardi community met and appointed three leading men of that congregation to carry an address of loyalty to the king. This was done with great solemnity and the Sephardi Jews of England were glad to learn, a little time later, that the king had accepted their address and had expressed kind words about them.

But the Sephardi Jews now formed only about a quarter of the Jews in England. The remainder were Ashkenazim. When these learnt that their Sephardi brethren had expressed their loyalty separately, they were distressed. They felt that they should have been invited to join them, so that the whole of English Jewry might appear as a united body in their address to the Crown.

The Ashkenazim informed the Sephardim of these feelings. It was then agreed that while the former should on this single occasion convey their loyal sentiments to the king separately, in the future Sephardim and Ashkenazim should join into a single body for dealing with all important matters affecting Jews. For this purpose a council called the London Committee of Deputies of British Jews was set up composed of members of both congregations.

The Board of Deputies, as this council came to be called, is now known all over the world and has rendered valuable services to the Jewish people during the two hundred and more years of its existence. Indeed, at its very beginnings, it was called upon to answer appeals for help and advice from places as far apart as Jamaica and Rome.

The beginning of King George's reign witnessed

the complete conquest of Canada, following the victory of General Wolfe over the French at Quebec. Among the members of General Wolfe's staff was an English Jew, Aaron Hart, who had the position of commissary and was in charge of supplies for the army. There were also a number of Jewish officers in the British army. Soon after the conquest, Jewish settlers came to Canada, residing mainly in Montreal. By 1768 there was a sufficient number of Jews to form a community, and in that year a congregation was set up under the name of *She-erith Yisrael,* which means remnant of Israel. Most of the members were Sephardim, and their synagogue therefore followed the Sephardi services and customs. The first two Scrolls of the Law used in this synagogue were gifts from Bevis Marks Synagogue in London.

The increase in the number of Jews in the remoter British possessions, as well as in England, speeded up the cultural life of the Jewish people in these parts. The most valuable means of spreading knowledge was, of course, that of the printing presses. At the beginning of the Jewish resettlement in England and emigration to the New World, Jews in those places depended for their prayer-books, their Hebrew Bibles and other books of Jewish learning on the printing presses of Europe. In Holland, in parts of Germany, Italy and in Bohemia, there were printing presses that produced these books which were sold in places as far apart as London, Montreal, New York and the West Indies. But as time went on the Jews in these places found it more convenient to produce their own Bibles, prayer-books, and books of Jewish learning and even to publish translations into the languages commonly used by them. These languages were not only English, but Spanish which was used by the Sephardim, and Yiddish by the very large number of East European Jews who formed a large portion of the new congregations.

From 1705 onwards, there was a growing stream of books brought out for the use of the Jewish congregations in England and other places under British rule. The greater number of these were prayer-books for the daily services, sabbaths, festivals and fasts. The earliest were published with Spanish translations, though some appeared only in Spanish, without Hebrew, for there were among the Marranos many who did not know the Hebrew language and prayed in the Spanish tongue. The first English translation, by Isaac Pinto, appeared in New York in 1766. In England, however, there was no English translation until 1770. In 1772 a Yiddish prayer-book was published in London. Many of these books are now very rare, and can be seen only in libraries, where they are much treasured. They bear witness to the piety and sturdy loyalty to the Jewish faith of the Jews of those days. Although but newcomers in a strange land, their first thought was to transplant Jewish culture from their places of origin and teach it to their children thus making sure that it would flourish.

One of the most devoted scholars who laboured to give his brethren in England a knowledge of Jewish teaching was David Levi who was born in London in 1742 and died in 1801. Although a poor man who earned his living first as a shoemaker and later as a hatter, he was the author of a number of very useful works. These included a translation into English of the Five Books of Moses, the prayers of the Ashkenazi and Sephardi Jews and the festival services. Ever ready to defend the Jewish faith against attack, he published a courageous and strong reply to one of these attacks by the famous Dr Priestley the discoverer of oxygen and a dissenting minister.

The synagogues were at this time the main centres of Jewish life. The congregations were proud of their houses of prayer and did their utmost to beautify them. There were by 1770 four main synagogues in London: the Sephardi house of prayer known popularly as Bevis Marks, the Ashkenazi Great Synagogue in Duke's Place, the Hambro', and the New Synagogues in Leadenhall

Sir Moses Montefiore

Benjamin Disraeli as a young man

Street and Creechurch Lane respectively.

The Duke's Place synagogue was by now the chief house of worship of the Ashkenazi Jews. It was enlarged in 1790 and continued to serve the Jews of all England as their central house of prayer until destroyed by German bombs in an air raid on London in 1941.

Duke's Place synagogue was at that time specially famous for its musical services. The *Chazan* or Cantor, was assisted by a trained choir and the synagogue was usually packed to over-flow by attentive congregations who often in-cluded English Christians who were attracted by the fine singing and solemn conduct of the service. One of the choir, Myer Lyon, achieved special fame. So beautiful was his voice that people flocked from all parts to hear him. On one occasion a Christian clergyman, the Rev Charles Wesley, brother, of the famous John Wesley, visited the synagogue. He was so deeply moved by Myer Lyon's singing of the *Yigdal* at the end of the Friday evening Sabbath service, that he later adapted the tune to a Wesleyan hymn. This became so popular, that many thousands of copies were sold throughout the country. Myer Lyon later became a great singer on the English stage under the name of Leoni. But he remained true to the Jewish faith and never appeared in any performance on the Sabbath or any festivals. He

M

finally became *Chazan* in Kingston, Jamaica, where he ended his days.

Occasionally the peaceful course of life in England was relieved by some sensation or unusual event. In 1777 there was a really remarkable happening when a little Sephardi boy, seven years of age, Moses de Paz by name, arrived from Gibraltar. He came alone, without parents or friends, on a ship which docked at London. The story of his adventures thrilled the Jews of England. His parents in Gibraltar had been baptized by force and the small boy resolved to escape to England, for he was determined to remain a Jew. He made his way to a ship bound for London. Here the Elders of the Sephardi synagogue gladly took care of little Moses. They placed him in kind Jewish hands and provided for all his needs and educated him in the Jewish faith.

Another and greater sensation, however, occurred in 1787 when Lord George Gordon a brother of the Duke of Gordon, gave up Christianity and embraced the Jewish faith. He became a very pious Jew, grew a beard in full observance of Jewish custom and learnt the Hebrew language. The conversion came as a great surprise, for Lord George Gordon had been a staunch champion of the Protestant faith and had led the anti-Popery riots of 1780. These are known in English history as the Gordon riots.

Lord George Gordon took the name of Israel bar Abraham on being received into the Jewish fold. He was a *Ger Zadik* – that is, a Righteous Stranger for he was a true and sincere convert to Judaism, observing all the rites and rules. When charged with uttering a libel against Marie Antoinette, queen of France, he appeared in court bearded and with covered head, he was ordered to remove his hat. He refused, declaring he was a pious Jew. When committed to Newgate prison, he continued to observe the Jewish faith, praying every morning in *talith* and *tephilin* and eating only kosher food. A *mezuza* was fixed on the doorpost of his room. He dreamed of leading the Jewish people out of exile and back to the Holy Land. On June 7th 1788, Israel bar Abraham died in Newgate prison, a firm believer in the God of Israel and an unwavering witness to the true faith.

By this time Jews were no longer strange and unknown to Englishmen. On page 120 it is related how English writers had for many years depicted Jews either as ridiculous figures of fun or as evil-hearted villains. Now, however, that Jews in large numbers lived in England openly as Jews, their Christian neighbours and acquaintances began to see them as human beings like themselves. In 1794, Richard Cumberland, one of the most popular writers of the period, produced a play called The Jew which, for the first time presented on an English stage a Jewish character who was kindly, loyal and honest. This made a deep impression and it was followed by similar plays by other writers.

It was about 1780 that Jews began to distinguish themselves in quite a new field, that of the boxing ring. The name of Daniel Mendoza became prominent in 1784 when he thrashed a pugilist known as Harry the Coal-heaver. It is not so much the fact that he had beaten a man so much bigger and heavier than himself, but Mendoza's quite new style of boxing that very soon brought him fame in the sporting world. Indeed, the period of scientific boxing as compared with the brutal rough-and-tumble, the slogging of the earlier period, is dated in the annals of boxing as 'from the rise of Daniel Mendoza'. From 1784 to 1820, Mendoza was the champion of English boxing and was known as the Star of the East. He fought thirty-two principal fights and was distinguished for courage, coolness and particularly for his boxing style. He wrote a book called The Art of Boxing.

Mendoza's success encouraged other London Jews to enter the ring. The most famous among them was Samuel Elias, known as Dutch Sam. Though not above medium height and weight, he was remarkably strong and was referred to as 'the man of the iron fists'. Every one of his fights was against boxers taller and much heavier than himself. Like Mendoza, he followed the scientific method and was the first to introduce the 'upper-cut' into boxing.

The Jewish boxers at this period formed a friendly group, often acting as seconds for each other. They were always proud of their Jewishness. The newspapers of the period were fair to them and ever ready to praise them for their prowess.

During this period there occurred some of the most important events not only in English history, but also in the history of Europe as a whole. These were the French Revolution in 1789 and the Napoleonic Wars. There were victories and defeats, times of crisis as well as of national triumph. The British Empire was being extended in many directions and the wealth of the country grew. Indeed it may be said that the greatness of the British Empire owed much to the events of that period. In all the main happenings, the Jews of England, though still few in number, played their part.

The City of London was the centre of the country's wealth and finances. The merchant-princes and bankers of the City helped largely in the growth of the Empire and in supplying the funds for conducting war against the king's enemies, building up the new industries that were arising throughout the country and helping in the growth of the new settlements in distant parts of the Empire. In this a number of Jews rendered valuable services. You have read of the fame of Samson Gideon in earlier years. Also in this period there were Jews who followed this example, and rose to even greater heights. Chief among these were the families of Goldsmid and Rothschild. It has been said that without them the government would have been hard pressed in the Napoleonic War. It was Nathan Meyer Rothschild, the founder of the family in England, who arranged for the payment of the Duke of Wellington's army in the Peninsular War. He even supplied the government with information of what was happening in Europe during the war, before the government's own messengers reached London, for these were the days before telephone and radio, and news came by special messengers on horseback and by boat.

Jews also played their part in the actual fighting, as well as in manning the defences of England when Napoleon threatened to invade the country. In 1803 the London Jews flocked to the militia, and their numbers in the forces were far above their proportion in the population. At Waterloo there was a number of Jewish officers under Wellington, while at Trafalgar Jewish seamen shared in Nelson's great victory. Lord Nelson himself was friendly with Abraham Goldsmid, a member of the family already mentioned. On one occasion the Admiral appointed a Jew of Gibraltar, Aaron Cardozo by name, to head a mission to the ruler of Oran, a province in North Africa.

In literature the name of Isaac D'Israeli became prominent. He was descended from a Marrano family which had settled first of all in Italy and later in England. He was the father of Benjamin Disraeli, who later became Lord Beaconsfield, twice Prime Minister of England. Isaac D'Israeli wrote several learned books, including a work entitled The Genius of Judaism. He was a member of the Sephardi synagogue at Bevis Marks for many years. In 1813, however, he quarrelled with the Elders of the synagogue and some years later withdrew completely from the Sephardi community. In 1817, while himself remaining a Jew, Isaac D'Israeli had his children baptized. Among them was Benjamin, the future prime minister, who was then thirteen years of age.

On 15th May, 1800, a Jew by the name of Dyte was instrumental in saving George III from injury and perhaps even from death. The king was on a visit to the Drury Lane Theatre. While he stood bowing from the Royal box, a man named Hatfield fired a pistol at him from close range. It happened that Dyte sitting close to Hatfield was quick enough to strike his arm and spoil his aim so that the shots lodged in the panelling above the king's head. Dyte was rewarded by the king and English Jews were very proud and happy that it was one of their number who had rendered so great a service.

The long reign of George III came to an end in 1820. During it the Jewish community had made great progress. There were now congregations not only in London but also in Liverpool, Manchester, Birmingham, Portsmouth as well as a number of smaller groups in most of the large towns and ports. George III himself had been friendly to Jews. This friendship was shown also by his sons, the royal dukes.

On April 3rd, 1809, the royal Dukes of Cumberland, Sussex and Cambridge honoured the Jews of England with a visit to the Friday evening Sabbath service at Duke's Place synagogue. It was a great occasion. The path to the synagogue was strewn with flowers and a special poem in Hebrew was sung in honour of the royal visitors.

GEORGE IV 1820–1830
And
WILLIAM IV 1830–1837

The Jews of England had by now gained a respected place in the life of the country. In number they were over 20,000 and had made their mark in various spheres and were helping to build up the new industries which so much enriched the land in the period that followed. As you have seen in the last chapter, they had come forward in defence of the country during the great war against Napoleon and they regarded themselves in every way as Englishmen. Nevertheless, there were still many rights which they could not enjoy for as persons holding positions of trust in the government and government services had to take a Christian oath, Jews found very many positions closed to them. They could not become judges, or sheriffs, or members of Parliament.

But the Jews were not alone in having these various honours and posts closed to them. The law was equally unfair to Roman Catholics and members of other Christian sects whose conscience did not allow them to take the oath of the Church of England. The struggle for these rights had been started by the Roman Catholics and other Christians many years before it was resumed on the accession of George IV. Eventually, in 1829, Roman Catholics and other Christians were freed from taking the Christian oath in the old form, and many positions hitherto closed to them were from that time opened to them. But this change brought no improvement for Jews. True there was a new oath in place of the old one. But it was one that no Jew could take, for every one taking up positions of honour and trust in the service of the government had to take the oath using the words 'on the true faith of a Christian'.

It is to the credit of Christian Englishmen that many efforts were made by them to put their Jewish neighbours in the same position as themselves. Gradually, one by one, various important positions were opened to Jews either by abolishing the oath, or changing it. In 1830 the Common Council of the City of London allowed Freemen of the City to take the oath in their own way. This enabled Jews to become members of the various livery companies and opened the way to most of the other honours in the City. In 1835 a well-known Jewish merchant, David Salomons, was elected sheriff of the City. But this position could not be held without his taking the oath 'on the true faith of a Christian'. Parliament came to the rescue and a Bill was passed making it possible for a Jew to hold the office of sheriff, though no other office in the City. Salomons, however, eager to press for Jewish rights, succeeded in being elected an Alderman but was not allowed to take his seat. It was not until 1845, in the reign of Queen Victoria, that the law was changed and all offices in the City thrown open to Jews. It is pleasant to record that David Salomons was again elected Alderman in 1845, triumphantly took his seat and was actually elected Lord Mayor in 1855. He was the first Jew to hold this high position.

With their rise in wealth and importance, English Jews came to the fore in new fields. One of the most striking of these was the case of Lewis Gompertz whose work helped in the creation of the Society for the Prevention of Cruelty to Animals. His love of animals and his passion for their humane treatment was rooted in his Jewish religious feelings and his knowledge of the teachings of the Rabbis. Since his day there is no civilized country without a society for the prevention of cruelty to animals. His teachings helped bring about a kindlier treatment of dumb creatures than was ever known before.

QUEEN VICTORIA 1837–1901

The long reign of Queen Victoria, which began in 1837, ushered in the period of greatest change in the life of the Jews of the British Isles. During this time British Jews finally took their position as citizens with full and equal rights. You have seen in the last chapter their gradual rise to importance in many walks of life. By now there were large numbers of Jews whose parents and grandparents had been born in England, brought up in the same schools as their fellow citizens and differing from their neighbours only in their faith.

The Jews of the British Isles now showed that they were not willing to be denied all the rights enjoyed by British citizens of the Christian faith. We have seen how Sir David Salomons had by his perseverance gained for Jews the right to positions of honour in the City of London, even to that of Lord Mayor. But the old oath ending with the words 'on the true faith of a Christian', which every member of Parliament was bound to take before he could vote in the House of Commons, still barred Jews from being members of Parliament.

The struggle to do away with the Christian oath in Parliament lasted from before the accession of Queen Victoria until 1858. On fifteen separate occasions in a period of twenty-five years the subject was debated in the Houses of Parliament, until the victory was finally won.]

The chief Jewish champions in the struggle were Sir David Salomons, Baron Lionel de Rothschild, and a number of Christian statesmen. In order to force Parliament to deal with the unfair position of the Jews, both David Salomons and Baron de Rothschild allowed themselves to be elected to Parliament by a large number of Christian voters who knew that they could not serve as Members of Parliament unless the Christian oath was changed.

Baron de Rothschild was twice elected as Member of Parliament for the City of London and on each occasion had to give up his seat when he refused to take the Christian oath. David Salomons was of sterner mettle. When he was elected the second time, he entered the House of Commons and insisted on staying and voting without taking the oath, although there was a law punishing every Member of Parliament with a fine of £500 for each time he voted without taking the oath. Although his action was unlawful at that time, David Salomons spoke and voted in Parliament on the very question of his right as a

Jew to represent the people of Greenwich who had elected him. There was a great uproar in the House of Commons. The speaker called on him to withdraw, while many members supported Salomons and stood shouting and waving their hands. At last he was escorted out of the House of Commons by the Serjeant-at-Arms.

While the efforts for full rights were going on, the Jewish population continued to grow both in numbers and influence. There came to the fore a number of notable Jews who served both Britain and the Jewish people faithfully and loyally. The most remarkable of these was Sir Moses Montefiore whose life without blemish and full of honour is like a fairy story. He was descended from a Sephardi family that hailed from Italy. His every deed and thought was for his Jewish brethren, not only in England, but for those who were persecuted in foreign lands. He was a man of great wealth which he poured out lavishly for the benefit of both Jews and Christians. It can be said that every event of his life seemed to aid him in his good deeds. In the early part of his life he became friendly with the Duchess of Kent, the mother of Queen Victoria. This, like other friendships was later of great benefit to the causes which he championed. Indeed, the sufferings of Jews in many lands were so great that Sir Moses

Montefiore was continually busied in their defence. In this he was notably aided by British statesmen and by the British public who showed constant sympathy for persecuted Jews in foreign lands.

One of Queen Victoria's first acts on ascending the throne was to knight Moses Montefiore. This honour marked him out as favoured by the queen who as a child had played in the gardens of his country house at Broadstairs. It helped him later in his work for his brethren. Specially dear to him was the welfare of the Jews in the Holy Land. Although travelling was difficult and dangerous in those days, he made seven visits to Palestine, the last at the age of ninety. As an English knight he was received with honour by foreign monarchs and ministers. But this was used by him in no spirit of vainglory, but in the service of his own people. When the Jews of Damascus were threatened in 1840, with massacre because of the old false and lying charge of using Christian blood, Sir Moses, publicly supported by Queen Victoria and the whole of the British people, journeyed to the Sultan of Turkey and received from him an order of protection for his Jewish subjects. He paid similar visits to the Czar of Russia, the Sultan of Morocco, and to Rumania. So greatly was he loved by all Jews, that wherever he went on his missions, he was received with marks of deepest respect and affection.

To this day Sir Moses Montefiore is remembered in the Holy Land for the benefits he brought, building schools, hospitals and acquiring land where Jews learnt to till the soil of their fathers. He bought the ground on which the tomb of Rachel stands, and erected the edifice which is now a landmark on the road from Jerusalem to Bethlehem.

Sir Moses Montefiore lived to the great age of one hundred and one years and at his death in 1885 he was mourned by Jews all over the world. In all his deeds he was greatly aided by his wife, Lady Judith. In her memory he founded at Ramsgate a college for the study of Hebrew learning.

The advance to great power and influence by Britain during this period was greatly due to the leadership of Benjamin Disraeli. The son of Isaac D'Israeli (see page 183) Benjamin Disraeli, born in 1804, was brought up as a Jew until the age of thirteen. In early youth he showed great brilliance as a writer. He had, however, set his mind on politics, and in 1837 was elected to Parliament, where his black curly hair and dark flashing eyes made him a striking figure. Despite his baptism, he was always regarded and referred to as a Hebrew, and, indeed, was always proud

Rufus Isaacs, First Marquess of Reading

Sir David Salomons

of his Jewish birth. He played a great part in the reform movements of the Tory party, eventually becoming prime minister, first in 1868, and again in 1874. It was he who put the seal on British rule in India by proclaiming it an Empire and Queen Victoria its first Empress. His foresight played a great part in securing the British route to India by acquiring the island of Cyprus and control of the Suez Canal. The latter he achieved through the help of the House of Rothschild.

THE MODERN PERIOD

We have now reached the time which may be said to mark the beginning of the period in which we now live.

For the Jews of the United Kingdom freedom and full equality opened the way to progress in every branch of human activity. For the first time in many centuries there was a large Jewish community which could freely enter every field of learning, trade and commerce, the army and navy, the civil services. Parliament and the highest offices under the Crown were open to them.

Full freedom, or emancipation as it is called, was granted to the British Jews in 1858. From that time onward they progressed without hindrance and rose to the highest positions in whatever branch of activity they chose.

The number of Jews in Britain increased more rapidly than at any time since the return under Cromwell. This increase was due to two main causes. The first was the fact that Jews in other parts of the world naturally wished to settle in a country where they would enjoy full freedom. The second cause was the spread of persecution and disorder in Europe, Jews being the first and main victims.

At first the growth of the Jewish population was steady, but not large enough to attract much notice. In those days there was no hindrance to anyone coming into Britain. The new arrivals settled down mainly in districts where Jews already lived. Most of them arrived without any means, and at first depended on their brethren for food, clothing and shelter. The greater number were deeply religious and many were learned men who had brought with them treasures of Jewish learning. They established their own little synagogues and Hebrew classes for their children in private houses. Very soon, despite their poverty, there was a flourishing Jewish religious life with which the older and wealthier congregations were hardly in touch.

The poverty of the immigrants led to the creation of the Jewish Board of Guardians for the Relief of the Jewish Poor (now the Jewish Welfare Board). It became a model institution which has been much admired and copied in other parts of the world. Its funds come from free-will gifts from Jews.

The Jews' Free School, which had grown out of Hebrew classes early at the end of the previous century, now provided education and even clothing free of all cost for large numbers of the children of the new immigrants. This was of great value, for in those days parents had to pay for the education of their children.

But the Jews of Britain did not rest satisfied with their own comfortable position as compared with their brethren in other countries. There was a constant demand for Jewish news from all parts of the world. The first real Jewish newspaper in England known as *The Voice of Jacob,* was published in 1841 and continued for five years. It was soon followed by *The Jewish Chronicle,* a journal which still appears and celebrated its hundredth birthday in 1941. The old copies of these papers present in a very colourful manner the romance of Jewish life. They brought together the Jewish news from distant parts. One can read in their pages reports of happenings in places as far apart as Cochin in India, where there is a community of black Jews, and Australia where Jews were beginning to share with fellow Englishmen in the building up of the great Commonwealth.

It was no longer possible for the separate Jewish synagogues in London to go each its own way. The duty of educating the children of the community, of attending to the supply of kosher food and of serving the needs of the Jewish poor in religious matters made it necessary for them to come together and unite for managing these affairs. In 1870 the large Ashkenazi congregations in London, with the help of the Rabbi of the Great Synagogue in Duke's Place, Dr Nathan Adler, set up what is now known as the United Synagogue. One result of this was that the Rabbi of the Duke's Place Synagogue became recognized from that time onward as the Chief Rabbi of all the Ashkenazi congregations in the British Empire.

Thus strengthened by such useful institutions, the Jews of Britain began to look around for means of helping their less happy brethren in other countries. For this purpose there was set up in 1871 a Society called the Anglo-Jewish Association. Its objects were to help in the protection of Jews who suffered persecution abroad, and to assist them by setting up schools and raising funds for their welfare. In this work the British Jews were greatly helped by those among them who had reached important positions. Sir Moses Montefiore was still a grand figure and active, despite his great age. The Rothschild family who gave generously to Jewish and Christian charities alike and raised British influence abroad, were always ready to assist their less happy brethren in other countries.

Jews were also beginning to take a prominent part in the study of the Law of England. In 1871 a Jew, Sir George Jessel became Solicitor-General, which made him a Minister of the Crown, the first practising Jew to hold high political office.

Sir George Jessel's career eventually brought him to the position of Master of the Rolls. If you look back to the early chapters, you will find a great deal about the Pipe Rolls which were the records of the Royal Treasury in olden days. The position of Master of the Rolls was a very ancient post of honour. In 1290, at the time of the Expulsion, could anyone have foreseen that over 500 years later a Jew would be in charge of the Chapel of the Rolls? This, originally the Chapel of the Domus Conversorum is now the site of the Public Record office in Chancery Lane.

In 1885, Lord Rothschild was made a peer, the first practising Jew to sit in the House of Lords. As a student at Cambridge, he was a close friend of the Prince of Wales who later became King Edward VII. Lord Rothschild's influence in high places and his great wealth were frequently at the service of Jews in all parts of the world, and more than once his personal help prevented a great deal of suffering.

It was fortunate for the Jews of Europe that their brethren in Britain had attained such full freedom and high honour. The time was fast approaching when a new wave of persecution abroad would drive tens of thousands to seek refuge in new lands.

SHORES OF REFUGE

The year 1881 is a most important date in the history of our time. It marks the beginnings of events which are still moving on, and the end of which even we, so many years later, cannot yet see. Ever since the great wars of Napoleon conditions in Europe had been unsettled. Although Napoleon was no more, the effects of the overthrow of great kingdoms were still felt. The feudal system had been destroyed in Europe, never to return, although here and there attempts were still being made by rulers and those around them to hold up the march of progress.

Throughout history, whenever such great changes occurred, it was always Jews who were the first to suffer. Those who were against progress knew that they could always turn aside public discontent from themselves by working up hatred against the Jews who lived in their midst.

And so it came about that in the more backward European countries where the feudal system was making its last stand, that Jews of that period felt the full brunt of persecution.

Then, as later, Germany was the centre for spreading vile lies and hateful sentiments against Jews. In 1881, a large number of prominent Germans signed a petition to the German Government asking for special laws against the Jews. Very soon this wicked move stirred the ignorant rabble. Jews were attacked in the streets and life became unsafe. Within a few weeks the hatred against Jews spread to Austria and Hungary, resulting in rioting and violence.

All this was but the beginning of still greater disaster and suffering. On March 13th, 1881, the Czar Alexander II of Russia, an enlightened monarch, was murdered.

Unhappily he was succeeded by Alexander III who was guided by ministers who hated the Jews, and these soon set about their evil plans. The turmoil in Germany and other parts of Europe spread to Russia and massacres, called 'pogroms', broke out. Suddenly the streets of many towns would be filled with labourers and peasants who invaded the Jewish quarters, burned down houses and synagogues and looted and murdered. Jewish blood flowed in many cities.

It soon became known that the Russian Jew-haters had arranged these pogroms so as to be able to pretend that the Russian people had made up their minds to get rid of the Jews and that special laws would have to be passed to satisfy the people.

Indeed, in May, 1882, the Russian government issued a set of laws which deprived the Jews of Russia of rights which they had enjoyed for many centuries. These have since come to be known as the May Laws. Jews were driven out of villages and capitals of provinces and allowed to live only in one special area known as the 'Pale of Settlement'.

But the persecuted Jews of Europe were no longer living in the Middle Ages when travel was difficult and there were no new lands in which to settle. The United States of America an open and sparsely populated continent welcomed immigrants. There were the great British Colonies, like Canada and Australia, anxious to fill their empty lands, as well as the vast areas of South America rich in natural resources with small populations. There were also the shores of Britain where there were already thriving congregations and men who had risen to high positions.

The Jews of Europe would not bow to persecution. They had in them the blood of many centuries of courageous men who refused to submit to tyrants. Time after time even in the Middle Ages, tens of thousands of Jews had gone forth with their families in search of freedom to live their own lives rather than bear the yoke of oppression.

It is no matter for wonder then that the year

1882 witnessed a vast new exodus of Jews from Europe.

From Russia, Hungary and Rumania, tens of thousands of Jews made their way to the free countries beyond the seas. Britain, being the nearest of the free lands to the Continent, attracted many of the refugees.

This new immigration brought great changes in the life of the British Jews. Until then the congregations were made up mainly of persons who had been either born in England or whose families had been settled for a long time in the land. Their occupations were connected chiefly with commerce and foreign trade. Their language was English as were their newspapers. The synagogues, apart from numbers of private houses of prayer, were stately and conducted on English lines.

The great flood of new immigrants changed all this in a short period. From 1882 until the end of the century tens of thousands of Jews entered England. They came mainly from the Russian Empire, although a considerable number arrived also from Germany, Austria, Hungary and Rumania. Most of them arrived penniless, even the cost of their journey being paid by Jewish organizations that were set up in the German ports on the North Sea. The language of the overwhelming number was Yiddish.

The new immigrants were deeply religious with a love of Jewish tradition, many of them with profound knowledge of Jewish learning. A great number brought with them their own crafts and trades. They settled wherever there were already small groups of Yiddish-speaking Jews, such as in the East End of London, Leeds, Manchester, Liverpool and Glasgow, as well as in some of the country towns.

Very soon scores of little synagogues usually named after the places in Europe from which the worshippers came had sprung up in the new Jewish districts. The life of these immigrants was indeed colourful, although not without much hardship.

In that period there was a great deal of poverty in Britain among the general population. The poor lived wretchedly. Their housing and clothing was of the meanest. It was rare for the ordinary workman to have a new suit of clothes. There was no such thing as public restaurants for ordinary working people such as are now so common in all cities. Furniture in the houses of working-class families was of the meagrest kind, rarely more than a wooden bench and a table. It was not unusual for families to sleep on the floor, or to be huddled together in a single bed. Though the British Empire stretched far and wide, masses of what was then called the 'lower classes' were indeed poverty stricken; many were homeless paupers.

The new immigrants began their lives in these isles much the same way as their poorer non-Jewish neighbours. Together with them they passed through a period of wretched poverty but through their thrifty ways, hard work and energy played their part in bettering the general conditions.

Of great importance in the improvement in living conditions for all was what is known as the 'mass-production' system. By this means articles of clothing, furniture and such-like could be produced so cheaply and so quickly, as to make it possible for ordinary people to enjoy what was before enjoyed only by a few. In the mass production of ready-made clothes, underwear, furniture and boots, Jews played the greatest part. Indeed, it may be said that by this they largely changed the face of English life. They gave employment not only to the many thousands of Jewish immigrants but also to very large numbers of their non-Jewish neighbours.

The life of this period is vividly protrayed in The Children of the Ghetto, written by Israel Zangwill, himself the son of parents who had come from Eastern Europe.

Among those who have since attained high positions in the service of Britain, in all fields of life, whether on the field of battle, in literature, the arts and commerce, the overwhelming number are descended from the great flood of immigration which started in 1882.

THE LOVE OF ZION

The same persecutions that had started the flood of Jewish immigration towards the lands of freedom also set alight a flame that had been smouldering in Jewish hearts for many centuries. Weary of endless suffering and journeying from land to land, a number of Jewish leaders in Russia resolved to take the first step to end the Jewish exile. This yearning for redemption had been in Jewish hearts ever since the destruction of the Jewish state eighteen hundred years before. Jews had always dreamt and prayed for the return to the Land of Israel, for their own home.

In 1882 in the Russian city of Kharkov a number of Jews banded themselves together in a society known as the Bilu, (made up of the initials of the Hebrew words, *Beit Yaakov lechu Venelchah,* which means 'O House of Jacob, come ye and let us go'). They planned to set up colonies in Palestine where Jews would work on the land. This movement came to be known as *Hovevei Zion,* the 'Lovers of Zion' – from it there arose a mighty movement which stirred the whole of the Jewish people to its depths, and later brought together the Jews of the world and the people of Britain for the task of restoring the Land of Israel to the People of Israel.

In England the Lovers of Zion movement found much support not only among the new immigrants, but also among some of the older settlers. The most notable of the latter was Colonel Albert Goldsmid, who was at the head of the movement in England. He was born of Jewish parents who had been baptized in the Christian faith. He had himself returned to Judaism. It was his work that resulted in the growth of the Jewish Lads' Brigade and its great popularity in the last century.

This growing desire to work for the restoration of the Land of Israel made a great leap forward in 1896 when Dr Theodor Herzl, whose name was destined to become immortal as the founder of what is known as Zionism, published his book entitled The Jewish State. Dr Herzl decided that England with its freedom and its love of the Bible was the country most likely to support Zionism. Indeed, long before him a number of Englishmen had written and worked for the restoration of the people of Israel to the Land of Israel. Men and women like Lord Shaftesbury, Benjamin Disraeli, George Eliot, in her book Daniel Deronda, Laurence Oliphant and many others had awakened interest in the subject.

Disraeli in his romantic novel Alroy, written in 1833, which should be read by every Jewish boy and girl, tells the story of one who set out to redeem the people of Israel. The hero of the novel, David Alroy, uses words which have since been expressed by many a Zionist.

Dr Herzl came to London in 1896, addressed a public meeting and discussed his plans for rebuilding the Jewish State with Jewish leaders like Israel Zangwill, Lord Swaythling, Claude Montefiore and Lord Rothschild. He also met leading British statesmen, the most notable being Joseph Chamberlain, a minister of the Crown. From that time onwards the Zionist movement began to spread in the United Kingdom. English Jews played a very important part in the early days of Zionism. They helped Dr Herzl with money, advice, and by introducing him to notable persons who could help the work forward. The British public, too, became interested in the idea of the restoration of the Jewish State.

Although Britain favoured the Zionist plans she was not in a position to help Jewish settlement in Palestine which was in the possession of the Turks. It remained so until 1917 when the land was conquered by a British Army. Nevertheless in 1903 the British government offered the Jews a part of East Africa for a Jewish settlement. Although this offer was not accepted because Jews

'Carrying the Law' by Sir William Rothenstein

Sir Herbert Samuel (The first Viscount Samuel) in the dress
uniform of High Commissioner for Palestine

30. 6. 20.

Received from
Major General Sir Louis Bo
one Palestine, complete.

E. & O. E.

Herbert Samuel

Sir Herbert Samuel's receipt for Palestine

decided to remain loyal to their ancient fatherland, the offer itself was an act which recognised the need of the Jewish people for their own homeland.

In 1897 Dr Herzl called together the first Zionist Congress, a gathering of Jewish leaders from all parts of the world. The Congress met at Basle, in Switzerland. There came to it also Jewish representatives from England; for Zionist societies had sprung up all over the country. The members of the Lovers of Zion movement now gave their fullest support to Dr Herzl. From that time onward Zionism in Britain grew so fast that within a few years it had more followers than any other Jewish movement.

The reign of Queen Victoria which opened with the knighting of Sir Moses Montefiore, ended with British Jews as a prosperous and powerful community. The new king, Edward VII, had during the long reign of the queen made many friends among Jews in prominent positions. Jews moved easily in the highest society. They had made their way not only in Britain, but also in the colonies. Sir Matthew Nathan was appointed Governor of the Gold Coast (now Ghana) in 1900, the first Jew to hold such a position. Four years later he was given a still higher post, being appointed Governor of Hong Kong.

The reign of Queen Victoria saw the swift

growth of the British Empire, and especially the rise of the great dominions beyond the seas. Many Jews figured in this growth. New Zealand had a Jewish Prime Minister, Sir Julius Vogel, who was at the head of the government of that Dominion in 1875, and again in 1876. In Australia Jews played their part in exploration, in the rise of the mining industry as well as in agriculture. Their abilities were also felt in positions of government. The Hon. V. L. Solomon became Prime Minister of South Australia in 1899. The same may be said of the then Dominions of South Africa and Canada. In the former, Jews were prominent in the early pioneering days and a certain Nathaniel Isaacs was among the first to explore the lands of the Great Zulu chief Chaka with whom he signed a treaty. In Canada, Jewish history goes back to the days of the Conquest by General Wolfe (see page 174). Since those days large numbers of Jewish immigrants had entered the country, establishing themselves as farmers or workers in the cities.

King Edward VII commenced his reign in the midst of the war of Great Britain against the Boers in South Africa. The Boer War as it is called brought evidence of the deep Jewish loyalty and readiness to fight and die for their country. Over two thousand British Jews, all volunteers, served in the Boer War; 114 are known to have been killed in action. The City of London Volunteers included so many Jews, that it was sometimes referred to as a Jewish unit.

The only dark cloud on the Jewish horizon during the happy reign of King Edward VII was the increasing sign that enemies of Jewry were beginning to spread their hatred against Jews, by pointing to the steady flow of Jewish immigrants into England, refugees who came to escape from the persecutions in Russia. In time these so far aroused the public feeling, that the British government appointed a special Committee to enquire into the facts and figures of Jewish immigration. As a result Parliament passed in 1905 what was later known as the Aliens Act. It put a stop to free immigration.

By the time the short reign of King Edward VII came to an end in 1910, Jews had risen to the highest pinnacle in the political affairs of the country. During the general election to Parliament in January, 1910, as many as fifteen Jews were elected, and three Jews became Cabinet Ministers. They were Mr Herbert Samuel, later Viscount Samuel, who became Postmaster-General; Sir Rufus Isaacs, later the Marquis of Reading and Viceroy of India, was appointed Solicitor-General; and Edwin Montagu, a younger son of Lord Swaythling, was appointed Secretary of State for India.

GEORGE V 1910–1936

Early in the reign of George V, the Jewish congregations of the British Empire were thrown into mourning by the death of the beloved Chief Rabbi Herman Adler who had been their religious guide since 1891. He was succeeded by Dr Joseph H. Hertz. The Jews of Britain were now filled with great anxiety because of the suffering of the Jews of Russia. In that country there had been many pogroms. Since the passing of the Aliens Act it was no longer possible for Jews to come to England freely. All that English Jews could do was to seek the aid of Britain for their suffering brethren as well as to raise money for sending the victims to lands beyond the seas. Britain was, however, in alliance with the Russian Empire. She was expecting war with Germany and was not able to act as vigorously as she had done in the past.

In May 1913, the Jews of Britain were greatly honoured when, Sir Rufus Isaacs, was made Lord Chief Justice, the first time a Jew had held such a position in these islands.

Peace was rudely shattered in 1914, by the outbreak of the First World War. Although this found Britain fighting on the same side as Russia which was utterly hated by every Jew because of its cruelty to Russian Jews, British Jewry came forward in great numbers to serve the country against the king's enemies. Sir John Monash, an engineer in Melbourne, Australia, rose to supreme command of the Australian forces in France. Sir Albert Stern helped develop the production of the first tanks, while yet another Jew, Solomon J. Solomon, an artist, perfected the art of camouflage. This is the art of so disguising places and objects, as to make them appear different to the enemy – or if moving objects, such as ships and lorries, to make direction of travel uncertain. A Jewish woman, Mrs Ayrton, perfected a fan for use against poison gas.

During the four years of the War, more than 50,000 Jews joined the British forces. Of these 8,920 were either wounded or killed in action. Five Jews gained the Victoria Cross, the highest award for valour. Forty-nine were decorated with the Distinguished Service Order; 85 with the Distinguished Conduct Medal; 612 with the Military Cross; 329 gained the Military Medal and eleven received the Distinguished Flying Cross; 528 Jews gained other decorations, and 336 were mentioned in despatches. It was a truly magnificent record of loyalty and courage.

It was during the first World War that the Zionist Movement which, as we saw, came into being towards the end of Queen Victoria's reign, made its greatest step forward. On November 9th, 1917, Jews in all parts of the world were roused to enthusiasm by the announcement that the British government promised to restore Palestine to the Jewish people after the defeat of the Turks who were fighting on the side of Germany. That announcement is known as the Balfour Declaration, after Mr Balfour who signed it in the name of the British Government. The Balfour Declaration brought in on the side of Britain Jews in all parts of the world. In America which had not yet joined Britain as an ally, Jews in great numbers crossed the border into Canada, to join the British forces.

Four months before the Balfour Declaration was published a great event had occurred. Britain had agreed to allow Jews to enlist in special Jewish battalions which were to be sent to Palestine to take part in the conquest of the Land of Israel. This was achieved largely through the efforts of Vladimir Jabotinsky, a man whose name has since become known as one of the greatest leaders of the Jewish people of recent times. When the Balfour Declaration was published, Jews from all parts of the world came to join the Jewish battalions and fight for Palestine. They came from places as distant as South America and Australia. This was the first time in nearly two thousand years that Jews were able to take up arms and fight in a Jewish force for their ancient fatherland.

At the end of the First World War in 1918, Britain held Palestine, and two years later Sir Herbert Samuel was appointed head of the government in Palestine with the title of High Commissioner. Jews throughout the world looked forward with hope that the country's rule by a British Jew of such distinction would bring about great and swift progress for the Jewish people in the land of their fathers. Unhappily, Sir Herbert Samuel's rule met with many setbacks, and in a short time it was seen that the Jewish restoration was not to be achieved as easily as was hoped.

Sir Herbert Samuel held the position of High Commissioner for Palestine till 1925. He was succeeded by High Commissioners who followed each other within periods of a few years.

The great hopes that seemed ready to blossom into lasting happiness for the Jewish people at the end of the World War, soon faded. In Palestine, Jews met with many difficulties. They found obstacles in the way of entering their ancient homeland, of buying land for settlement and many other difficulties. Very soon, also, in Europe dark clouds loomed. In Germany, Jew-baiters began to blame

Jews for the German defeat in the war. The cruel Adolf Hitler came to the fore in 1924 as the leader of these Jew-haters. He preached complete destruction of the Jewish people and organized the young and the old against them. And so fast did the movement of Adolf Hitler grow, that within a few years life became unsafe for Jews in Germany, and the hatred spread also into neighbouring lands.

By 1933, Hitler's teachings gained so much support that his followers took over the government of Germany, and Hitler the arch-enemy of all Jews became the ruler of the country.

From 1935 onwards a new flood of Jewish emigration out of Europe began. Tens of thousands of Jews dreading massacre and pillage, left Germany and made their way into neighbouring countries. There, too, they were not allowed to stay, but had to move on. Tragic Jewish history was repeating itself. Britain opened its doors to tens of thousands of German-Jewish refugees. Others made their way to America. Many thousands found their way to Palestine, braving the elements in order to reach the Land of Israel.

Hitler's cruelty knew no bounds. Having chosen Jews as his first victims, he looked round for others. He first seized Austria, then Czechoslovakia. In both these countries his first step was to attack Jews, rob them of their belongings and put them to flight. But the time was fast approaching when Britain and others were to call a halt to Hitler's ambitions which now began to threaten even Britain.

In 1939 Hitler attacked Poland, and thereby started the Second World War in which the British Empire found herself ranged with France and Poland against Germany and a number of smaller European states who followed in her wake.

1939–1945

Britain was ill-prepared for war. While Germany had been arming, Britain had tried by peaceful means to turn Hitler aside from his ambitions. So it came about that when war broke out, the people of Britain suffered many a setback and many a weary month of anguish until the turning of the tide.

At the call of duty every man and woman rallied to the flag which stood for freedom. The Jews of Britain, with the cruelties of Hitler in their minds, responded magnificently. In all the armed forces and civilian defence against air-raids they stood shoulder-to-shoulder with their fellow Britons.

The first brutal attacks by the German air force on London very often found their targets in Jewish districts. The great German air-raids of 1940 and 1941 devastated the Jewish district in East London, apart from heavy attacks in the North London area where many hundreds of Jews lost their lives. Also in other parts of the country, such as Manchester, Liverpool and Glasgow, Jews suffered heavily. Jewish men and women serving in the Civil Defence were prominent among those decorated for valour. The first person to gain the award of the British Empire Medal for bravery was a Jewish girl telephonist who remained on duty after a bomb had struck the building in which she was stationed. The George Cross and George Medal were won by Jewish men and women for distinguished service during air-raids.

Up to 1944 many synagogues were destroyed by German bombs, among them the 222 year old Great Synagogue in Duke's Place, which was completely burnt out, leaving an empty shell.

In the armed services many hundreds of Jews were decorated, and Jewish names were cited for valour in every one of the Services. Never before were there so many Jews serving in the British Army, or so many in the high ranks of all three services.

Since 1917, when the Balfour Declaration was published, Jews had become a power in Palestine. Although the country was not yet restored to the Jewish people there were already 500,000 Jews in Palestine when war broke out in 1939. Like their fellow Jews in Britain, they responded to the call. By the second year of the war about 30,000 Jews of Palestine were in the British forces. A great number of them were in all the battles that led to the liberation of Abyssinia and the great battles that brought about the defeat of the Germans in North Africa. At the decisive battle of El Alamein it was the fortifications built by the Jewish engineers from Palestine that helped to save the day when the outcome was in doubt. At Tobruk, Jewish companies from Palestine fought together with Australians, New Zealanders and South Africans during the long siege. Later, Jewish soldiers from Palestine were among the first to enter the re-conquered cities of North Africa, and to greet their brethren who had been for long under the German heel.

As in the First World War, the Jews of Palestine as well as those of other countries, offered to raise a great Jewish army to fight under the Jewish flag on the side of Britain. This was not accepted by Britain, although she agreed to allow a separate Jewish battalion to be formed by the Jews of Palestine, and later established the Jewish Brigade Group which fought under the Jewish banner as part of the British army.

CONCLUSION

When the war came to an end in 1945, there was revealed the terrible story of the murder of nearly 6,000,000 Jews by the Nazis. The greater part of the Jews in Europe had been seized and placed in prison camps to be tortured and done to death in a manner even worse than had happened in the Dark and Middle Ages.

But as though to fulfil the words of our ancient Prophets who always warned us against despair even in the darkest hour, the destruction in Europe was followed by the most dramatic event in our history since the destruction of the second Temple in Jerusalem.

Less than three years after the end of the Second World War, the State of Israel once again miraculously came into being. After difficult times and desperate days of which you are bound to read in a general history of our people, the Jewish State was proclaimed on May 15, 1948. After 2,000 years the whole of the period covered by our history in Exile, the Land of Israel was once again under Jewish government. With every confidence Jews throughout the world welcomed the rebirth of the State of Israel as a sign that the long and dark night of Exile had at length ushered in the bright dawn of a happier future for our people.

Here, in Britain, Jews continued to play their part in promoting and working for the welfare of the country. Much had to be done to repair the ravages and losses resulting from the Second World War. In every walk of life, in the professions as well as in business, Jews proved themselves worthy and loyal citizens. Today, as never before in the history of our people in this land, they occupy prominent and leading positions. There are many titled Jews and 23 Jewish peers sit in the House of Lords; while in the House of Commons Jewish Members of Parliament number 40. There is scarcely an office of the Government's Civil Service without a Jew.

There has been a marked improvement in the relations between Jews and Christians. During the 1939–45 war the Council of Christians and Jews was formed to establish friendly understanding. Talks and lectures were held alike in synagogue and church. In 1966 this reached a high point with the holding in Westminster Abbey of an exhibition, 'The Corner of the Earth', to mark the 900th anniversary of Abbey's foundation, as well as to pay tribute to Anglo-Jewry from its early beginnings in the reign of William the

Conqueror. The title of the exhibition is taken from the pun '*Angle*-terre', the French name for Britain which means angle, or corner of the world. Thus the medieval Jewish writers called Britain in their Hebrew writings.

But the most momentous and striking event for English Jews as well as to Jews the world over, has been the victory of Israel against the surrounding Arab countries, in June 1967. After 2,000 years of our people's varied history, Jerusalem the Holy City is once more Jewish. After a lightning war of six days, in which Israel stood alone, unaided by any other country, surrounded on all sides by enemies bent on Israel's complete destruction, Prophecy was fulfilled. By a miracle as wondrous as any in our Bible, Israel emerged victorious. Today in Jerusalem as over the rest of the Holy Land the blue and white flag flies proudly.

At the time of crisis, when Israel like Britain in 1940 stood alone, Jews from all over the world flocked to offer their services and help. In Britain, as elsewhere, many, young and old alike, proved their worth and played their part so that in Israel's victory, all Jewry has a share.

Ending this history, and looking back on the long story of Jews in Britain, we realise that nearly a thousand years have passed since Jews first began to impress their mark on the British

Isles. During that long period there have been times of great stress, as well as of joy. It may be said that for nearly a thousand years there was never a period when Jews were wholly absent from the country. As the darkness of the Middle Ages passed away and the age of freedom dawned, so Jews began to come into their own and to claim and receive the treatment of equal citizens. With the enjoyment of the rights came also the duties of citizenship. Eagerly, indeed, did British Jewry press forward into the public service of the country. In war and peace, in Parliament and the ordinary pursuits of commerce and industry, they played their part in the progress and rise of Britain. Over the many centuries British Jewry looks back with pride on the past, and with hope and confidence in the future.